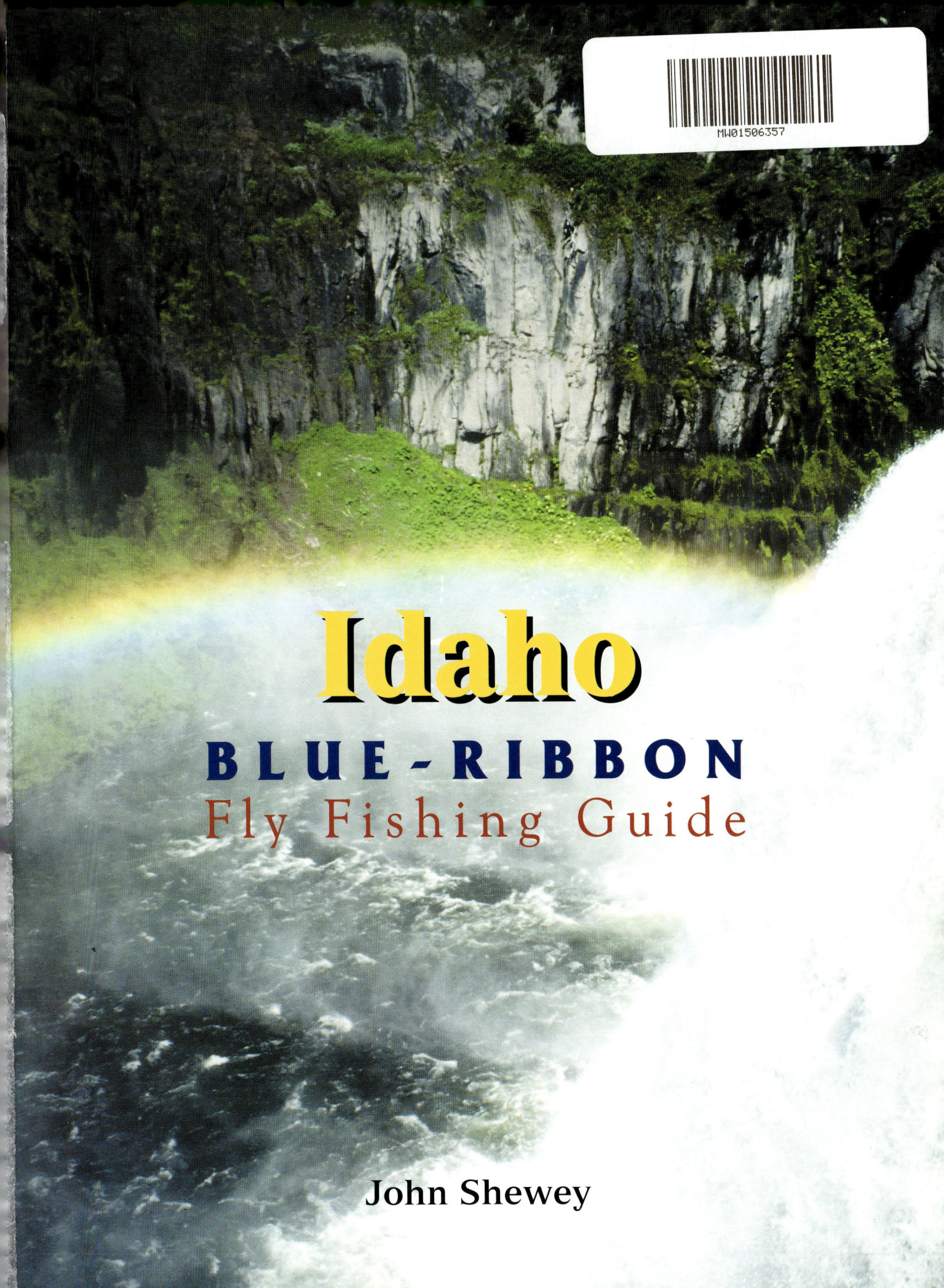

Idaho

BLUE-RIBBON

Fly Fishing Guide

John Shewey

Idaho

BLUE-RIBBON

Fly Fishing Guide

John Shewey

Frank Amato PORTLAND

ABOUT THE AUTHOR

A writer, author and photographer from Oregon, John Shewey travels extensively throughout the Northwest in pursuit of fly-angling adventures. Summer steelhead and upland gamebirds occupy much of his time during the autumn, but John's angling pursuits lead him annually to destinations ranging from the Pacific surf to the famous Western spring creeks to the the alpine lakes of the West. His steelhead flies have earned national recognition. John has authored numerous magazine articles and his other books include *Mastering the Spring Creeks*, *Fly Fishing for Summer Steelhead*, *Northwest Flyfishing: Trout & Beyond*, *Fly Fishing Pacific Northwest Waters*, *Alpine Angler*, and *North Umpqua Steelhead Journal*.

ACKNOWLEDGMENTS

This project would not have been possible if not for the assistance of many individuals. My sincere thanks go to the people of the Idaho Department of Fish & Game, especially Ned Horner, Richard Scully and Steve Yundt. I also wish to thank Dave Tucker and Jimmy Gabettas for fact-checking significant parts of the manuscript. Dave Tucker also tied most of the trout flies in this book and his masterful tying skills are very much in evidence herein. Thank you also to Dave Burns of McCall, whose skilled hands supplied many of the unique and exquisite steelhead patterns for the book. Bruce Staples deserves thanks as well for the helpful historical information about eastern Idaho flies in his fine book *Snake River Country*. Thanks also to my fishing partners, Forrest Maxwell and Tim Blount, who have helped immensely in my "field research" (and loved every minute of it).

Published in 1999 by:
Frank Amato Publications, Inc.
PO Box 82112 • Portland, Oregon 97282 • (503) 653-8108

Softbound ISBN: 1-57188-135-2   Softbound UPC: 0-66066-00335-5

Cover photo: Frank Amato
Frontispiece photo: Frank Amato
Title Page photo: John Shewey
Back Cover photo: John Shewey
Fly Plates: Jim Schollmeyer
All other photographs taken by the author unless otherwise noted.

Book Design: Tony Amato
Cover design: Amy Tomlinson

Printed in Canada

1 3 5 7 9 10 8 6 4 2

TABLE OF CONTENTS

Map **6**

Introduction **8**

GREG THOMAS

GREG THOMAS

FRANK AMATO

GREG THOMAS

93

94   96

91
92 ● Coeur d' Alene

95

90

90

5   88

85
87
● Lewiston

87

89

89

54 60 56
51 55   53   75   79
52   74
57   63   77
67   59 61   62
58
4   76
66 65   80   78
64
70 81 82
69   44
68   45   38   40
42   41 37
43   39   21
71   20   19
47   3   19   Idaho Falls ●   1
46 Twin Falls   24   Pocatello ●

50   25 26   2

Boise ●

9
2 3
4 10
5
1   6 16 17
18 7
8   15
14
11   13
11
11
12

27 28
23
22
30
30 36
29 34 35
31 33   32

72
73
49 48
49

Upper Snake Region 1

1 Henry's Fork
2 Henry's Lake Outlet
3 Coffeepot Reach
4 Box Canyon
5 Harriman Park
6 Riverside to Warm River
7 Warm River to Ashton
8 Ashton to Chester Backwaters
9 Henry's Lake
10 Island Park Reservoir
11 South Fork Snake
12 Palisades Reservoir
13 Teton River, Valley Stretch
14 Teton River, Canyon Section
15 Fall River
16 Warm River
17 Robinson Creek
18 Sand Creek Ponds
19 Big Lost River
20 Little Lost River
21 Birch Creek

Southeast Region 2

22 Blackfoot River
23 Portneuf River
24 Fort Hall Bottoms
25 Daniels Reservoir
26 Hawkins Reservoir
27 Chesterfield Reservoir
28 24-Mile Reservoir
29 Treasureton Reservoir
30 Bear River
31 Preston/Malad City Area Warm-water Reservoirs
32 Bear Lake
33 Cub River
34 Bloomington Lake
35 St. Charles Creek
36 Little Valley Reservoir

Magic Valley Region 3

37 Silver Creek
38 Big Wood River
39 Bear Tracks Preserve, Little Wood River
40 Little Wood Reservoir/Fish Creek Reservoir/Lava Lake
41 Magic Reservoir
42 Little Camas Reservoir
43 Mormon Reservoir
44 Baker Lake
45 South Fork Boise River (above Anderson R. Res.)
46 Hagerman Wildlife Management Area
47 Billingsly Creek (Hagerman Valley)
48 Jarbridge River
49 Bruneau River
50 Sublett Reservoir

Southwest & Salmon Regions 4

Southwest Region, North Half

51 Little Payette Lake
52 Lake Fork Creek
53 South Fork Salmon River and Tributaties
54 Little Salmon River
55 High Lakes of the Payette/ South Fork Salmon Drainage
56 Upper Payette Lake/ Upper North Fork Payette River
57 Middle North Fork Payette River
58 Sagehen Reservoir
59 Horsethief Reservoir
60 Brundage Reservoir
61 Deadwood Reservoir
62 Sulphur Creek
63 Bear Valley Creek
64 South Fork Payette River
65 Middle Fork Payette River
66 North Fork Payette River
67 Weiser River Drainage

Southwest Region, South Half

68 South Fork Boise River
69 Middle Fork Boise River
70 North Fork Boise River
71 C.J. Strike Reservoir
72 Owyhee River
73 Sheep Creek Reservoir/ Mountain View Reservoir

Salmon Region

74 Lemhi River
75 Middle Fork Salmon River
76 Upper Salmon River (Stanley Basin to Corn Creek)
77 Frank Church River of No Return Wilderness
78 Pahsimeroi River
79 Williams Lake
80 Bayhorse Lakes
81 Sawtooth Wilderness
82 White Cloud Peaks

Northern Idaho Clearwater & Panhandle Regions 5

83 Lochsa River
84 Kelley Creek
85 North Fork Clearwater
86 Selway River
87 Clearwater River
88 Little North Fork Clearwater River
89 Main Salmon River (Corn Creek to mouth)
90 St. Joe River
91 North Fork Coeur d'Alene River
92 Spokane River
93 Moyie River
94 Priest Lake/Upper Priest Lake
95 St. Maries River
96 Pack River

GREG THOMAS

INTRODUCTION

In writing this guide book I had to consider many potential conse-
quences. Chief among these is that by writing about specific destinations I would likely make somebody mad. After all, none of us likes
to see our "pet" waters written up in either book or magazine form. My
answer to this was simply to focus on the most significant waters—those
waters of most interest to fly anglers. In the case of small waters in out-
of-the-way places, I decided in many cases to offer enough comment to
get you started in the right direction. For other such waters, I have said
little or nothing: Anyone with a desire to explore new places can locate a
tiny mountain stream or a remote alpine lake on a Forest Service map,
lace up the hiking boots, and embark on a voyage of discovery. You don't
need my help to do that.

I have not visited every destination listed in this book. I have been to
most of them. Those places to which I have not personally ventured,
however, received the same thorough research as those with which I am
familiar. My goal, above all else, was to write an accurate and useful guide
to the many great trout waters in Idaho. Though I have not lived in Idaho
since the 1970s, I am in the unique position of being as familiar as any fly
angler with the myriad waters of the Pacific Northwest as a whole.

Over the past 20 years I've spent a lot of time wandering the West,
especially Idaho, Oregon and Washington. Of the three, I have no doubt
that Idaho offers the most varied, most productive, and most beautiful
trout waters. That is not to slight Oregon and Washington, for they too
boast of countless great trout destinations and many splendid steelhead
rivers. But Idaho is a special place: Its population growth has lagged far
behind its two neighbors to the west, so you can still find a great trout
stream all to yourself.

Within this guide I hope you will find information that will help you
discover Idaho from a fly angler's perspective. Writing this book was a
great experience for me, I visited waters I have always wanted to fish and
re-acquainted myself with old stomping grounds, rekindling fond
memories of great days afield.

UPPER SNAKE REGION

Idaho's Upper Snake region features a special blend of world-renowned fly angling destinations and little-known, but high-quality trout waters. The famous waters of this part of Idaho are indeed storied fisheries: The Henry's Fork, Henry's Lake and the South Fork of the Snake. But lesser-known waters like Fall River, Teton River, Big Lost River and Island Park Reservoir offer excellent fly angling opportunities.

This is a diverse region, its diversity a product of the area's unique geography. Island Park—the corner of Idaho wherein lies the famed Henry's Fork—is essentially one huge volcanic caldera. The Henry's Fork is born of waters emanating from Henry's Lake and from voluminous natural springs. After winding through the green meadows of the Island Park country, the Henry's Fork plunges off the ancient caldera and continues southward, picking up the waters from Warm River, Fall River, the Teton River and others before meeting the South Fork north of Idaho Falls. After leaving the high country, the Henry's Fork and its tributaries form the basis for the agricultural economy of the upper Snake River Plain. This is Idaho's potato country and it is the river that makes the entire economy possible.

The South Fork, meanwhile, derives its headwaters from the high granite crags of the Teton Range in Wyoming. Before the river crosses the state line it has already formed a substantial presence, but its flow is immediately tamed by 16,000-acre Palisades Reservoir. Below the reservoir, the South Fork becomes a world-class fishery for cutthroat and brown trout, its stonefly and caddis hatches rivaling those of the best rivers in the Rocky Mountain region.

The central and eastern part of the Upper Snake region offers stark contrast to the water-rich river valleys of extreme eastern Idaho. Once you leave the comfortable confines of the Snake River Plain and travel beyond the reaches of irrigation-based agriculture, you see a very different part of this diverse state. You find desert. Sagebrush dominates the barren expanses of a basin desert whose oddly placed buttes and brutal lava fields define rugged vastness.

Water is at a premium and there isn't much to go around. The Big and Little Lost rivers are so named because they meander out into the desert and disappear. That portion of their flow that has not been trapped and diverted by agriculture in the valleys above or evaporated in the dry desert sun, begins a new journey underground. The name "sinks" is appropriately applied to the areas where the rivers sink beneath the surface.

Both the Big Lost and Little Lost rivers drain spectacular mountain ranges to the north and northwest of the desert. The Little Lost, in fact, gathers its headwaters from the east side of the Lost River Range, which includes Idaho's tallest peaks in 12,662-foot Mt. Borah and 12,228-foot Leatherman Peak. The Big Lost, similarly originates in the beautiful Boulder and Pioneer Mountain ranges.

The Henry's Fork is renowned for its big rainbows and its dry-fly fishing.

FRANK AMATO

A white pelican takes flight.

This sprawling desert towards which the Lost Rivers flow is a curious land. Craters of the Moon National Monument offers a close-up look at dramatic volcanic lava flows and formations. Take the time to explore the area if you're in the vicinity. Craters of the Moon encompasses just a small part of a gigantic lava field. Farther east you enter lands administered by the Idaho National Engineering & Environmental Laboratories (INEEL) where nuclear testing and engineering work is carried out in a rather secretive environment. INEEL employs lots of people from Idaho Falls and the surrounding areas and they travel to and from the site by bus each morning and evening—these are the best times to avoid traveling Hwy. 20 between INEEL and Idaho Falls.

A final note: the Free Fisherman's Breakfast is served up at the park in St. Anthony every year on the Friday before Opening Day (the Friday prior to Memorial Day weekend). As a youngster I lived just a few blocks up the street from the big event and I can still taste those warm flapjacks to this day. Rumor has it that the Fisherman's Breakfast has grown since then—thousands attend annually.

Super-dense hatches offer world-class dry-fly fishing on the Henry's Fork. Crippled and stillborn blue-winged olives that piled up along a weed line during one afternoon hatch.

Henry's Fork

Amongst the world's most renowned fly angling destinations, the Henry's Fork of the Snake River boasts tremendous hatches and sophisticated trout, the combination of which challenges the most experienced of fly fishers. At the same time, this fertile river offers something for everyone, for it is the flat-water sections of Harriman Park that are known for difficult fish. The remaining reaches of the Henry's Fork provide excellent fishing for trout that may or may not prove difficult at any given time.

The Harriman Park section spans more than seven miles, from the town of Last Chance downstream to the Osborn Springs reach east of Hwy. 20. Upstream from Last Chance, the river flows from Island Park Reservoir into Box Canyon, whose steep, boulder-strewn length creates a haven for big rainbows in waters that are often difficult to fish. Below the glassy waters of Harriman Park, the river again gathers momentum for a rapid descent off the Island Park Caldera. Numerous rapids and three major waterfalls create a scenic cascading river whose waters hold many trout, many of the larger specimens inhabiting areas that are generally left alone by the majority of anglers.

After leaving Island Park country, the Henry's Fork is joined by the Warm River at Stone Bridge. Here the Henry's Fork becomes a valley river, surrounded by the workings of southeast Idaho's agricultural industry. Despite being dammed at Ashton and despite suffering from the water quality changes that always accompany such places, the lower Henry's Fork still offers some fine fly angling between Stone Bridge and St. Anthony.

Henry's Lake Outlet

Historically, Henry's Lake Outlet flowed through private lands and thus allowed little opportunity for fly anglers to ply its waters for cutthroat, hybrids and brook trout that escaped from the lake above. However, In April of 1994, The Nature Conservancy purchased the 1,450-acre Flying R Ranch, now called Flat Ranch. The Conservancy's goal is to restore winter flows to the upper Henry's Fork in an effort to restore the year-round vitality of this long-neglected system. The Conservancy is now working in conjunction with the Henry's Lake Foundation, the Henry's Fork Foundation and private landowners in the area to accomplish the long-term goal of restoring and protecting the watershed.

The Nature Conservancy's acquisition of Flat Ranch, which includes four miles of riverfront property, has opened this reach to public access. Fly anglers should keep an eye on this water in future years as it will likely develop into a top-notch trout stream. The Nature Conservancy of Idaho has been directly responsible for saving, restoring, and preserving some of Idaho's significant fly angling destinations, among them famed Silver Creek. Anglers wishing to support the efforts of The Nature Conservancy can contact the Idaho Field Office at P.O. Box 165, Sun Valley, Idaho 83353.

Coffeepot Reach

The section of river from Upper Coffee Pot Campground down to McCrea Bridge at the top of Island Park Reservoir produces some big trout that move up from the reservoir to spawn or to feed on kokanee eggs. Otherwise, the trout in this section are a mix of small wild fish and keeper-sized hatchery plants. The campground section, of course, is heavily fished, but Coffee Pot Rapids a short distance below is more difficult and requires a short hike. An occasional big reservoir fish rewards anglers skilled enough to thoroughly work these fast, boulder-strewn narrows. (These rapids make this section of the river unflotable).

Box Canyon

In stark contrast to the placid waters of Harriman Park, the 3-1/2-mile-long Box Canyon reach of the Henry's Fork is characterized by fast, boulder-strewn runs, riffles, and extensive deep pocket water. Some huge rainbows live in this section, with fish up to 10 pounds being taken on occasion by fly anglers. Rainbows from 14 to 20 inches are common.

Most of the fishing in Box Canyon is done with streamers and large nymphs. Woolly Buggers, sculpin patterns, stonefly nymphs and other such beasts are effective. Dry-fly anglers take heart, though, because "The Box" has its moments when stoneflies and caddis bring trout to the surface. The stoneflies (salmonflies and goldens) hatch during early summer and at the same time some prolific caddis emergences occur. Hopper fishing can be good during late summer.

Many anglers choose to float Box Canyon. The drift is short and floaters can continue on down to Harriman if they so desire. Just about any craft can make the float, with drift boats being the odds-on favorite. Kick boats are becoming more and more popular here as elsewhere, but watch out for boulders and sweepers. The put-in is located just below Island Park Dam and the first take-out is located at the bottom of the canyon near Last Chance (below the cabins). To get to the ramp below the dam, turn west on Island Park Dam Road just north of Pond's Lodge.

Walk-in traffic in Box Canyon is fairly heavy and numerous trails descend into the canyon from the rim above. Box Canyon Campground is a good starting point, but there are a couple of roads that approach the

The beginning of Box Canyon.

rim below the Buffalo River confluence. The wading in Box Canyon has a reputation for being rather nasty and it can be just that. But to keep things in perspective, you'll find Box Canyon a piece of cake if you've spent time on the South Fork of the Boise during high summer flows or better yet on Oregon's Deschutes or North Umpqua. A pair of stream cleats or cleated wading boots can tame Box Canyon considerably.

Harriman Park

Granted to the state of Idaho by the Harriman family in 1977, the tremendous acreage known as Harriman Park or Railroad Ranch offers some of the greatest dry-fly fishing one could hope to find anywhere. The rainbows in this reach get a regular working over all season long by the myriad fly anglers who wade the placid waters of this most famous of dry-fly destinations.

By a combination of dense hatches, smooth, flat waters and fishing pressure, the rainbows of the Railroad Ranch become increasingly difficult to fool as they grow older and older. Trout spanning 16 to 20 inches are common, but are generally not easy. It is precisely this challenge that draws most Railroad Ranch regulars back to the river year in and year out.

Brown Drake.

Anglers visit Harriman Park to test their skills against some
of the world's most selective trout.

these hatches arrive on a predictable schedule every year, allowing fly anglers to plan trips around favorite hatches.

Access to Harriman Park is quite good, although a fair amount of walking is involved in some areas (typically the least crowded areas). Anglers can get to the river with ease as it flows past Last Chance along Hwy. 20 (a public parking area is located along the river on the southwest corner of town).

Another good access point is Osborn Bridge, under which the river passes after making a five-mile-long horseshoe bend past the old ranch buildings two miles west of the highway. Green Canyon Road, which turns west off the highway just south of Osborn Bridge leads to the old ranch buildings, where one can access the river's west bank. Watch for a sign announcing Harriman Park just west of the highway on Green Canyon Road. Just after making the right turn on to the entrance road you will find another parking area off to the right. A trail leads along the west bank from here, but my preference is to head north to the river and wade both channels to the east bank.

About two miles north of Osborn Bridge on Hwy. 20 you will see another parking area opposite the old driveway into the ranch. The road is gated, but you can make the mile-and-a-half walk to the river, ending up about dead center between Osborn Bridge and the north extent of the park near Last Chance. (This parking area is at the turnoff for Mesa Falls Scenic Route or State Route 47).

The Mesa Falls Scenic Route also leads down river to Osborn Springs. Head southeast on 47 about four miles until you see a sign announcing Osborn Springs. Turn right on the gravel road and then left when the road forks. You will emerge from the sparse lodgepoles, come over a rise and (after about two miles) arrive at the river. Form here you can fish both directions.

A few words on technique are perhaps in order for those who have never fished spring creek waters: Success on the large trout of Harriman Park consistently requires that you think in terms of hunting and stalking rather than fishing. Forget about blind casting to good looking water or to clusters of rising trout. Pick out an individual trout. Large trout can frequently be identified by their telltale gulping rises where little more than a big snout appears above the water's surface.

Having found a target trout, carefully position yourself to make a short, accurate cast. The ideal position leaves you *upstream* of and a rod's length or so opposite the fish. This position allows you to make a downstream cast so the fish sees the fly before the tippet. More importantly, perhaps, the upstream position allows you to correct for less-than-perfect casting accuracy by simply dragging the fly into the trout's feeding lane and then dropping the rod tip, and/or shaking out slack line to achieve a short drag-free, fly-first drift over the fish. If the trout doesn't rise for your fly, skate the fly off to the side and try again and again until you time one just right to coincide with that moment when the fish is ready to rise again.

Coupled with technique and careful approach is the need to choose the right fly to imitate the foods on which a particular trout is feeding. Compound hatches—several types of insects emerging simultaneously—occur frequently on the Henry's Fork and individual trout will respond in individual ways. One fish may feed exclusively on one stage of one insect while another trout may feed on everything that drifts over. Generally, most trout will feed selectively during dense hatches or spinner falls, requiring that you first identify the feeding strategy of your target trout and then choose the appropriate fly.

I think it's safe to assume that floating emerger and cripple patterns often out-fish upright-wing dun patterns for mayflies. Downwing caddis patterns, along with floating emerger patterns, out-fish standard caddis adult dressings. There exists no perfect fly for every encounter on a spring creek like the Henry's Fork, but some patterns perform better than others often enough to warrant their reputation as effective choices: A good example is the Floating Nymph, which will consistently produce better than just about any other dressing during hatches of small bluewinged olives. For a thorough treatise on spring creek techniques, see *Mastering The Spring Creeks*, published by Frank Amato Publications, Inc.

Numbers of trout are meaningless. What matters is the opportunity to "hunt" large trout, first locating a rising fish, then determining which insect (and there may be many) is falling prey to that trout, next stalking into position and finally making the perfect presentation—all the while knowing that a single mistake means failure.

The intensity of each encounter counts far more than the number of chances and although this kind of fishing may not appeal to all fly anglers, everyone should try this river at least once. Moreover, every fly angler deserves a chance to fish this famous destination at least once.

The hatches themselves are worth the trip. The mayflies are spectacular, with certain species offering such dense hatches that a feeding trout won't move more than an inch or two from side to side. What's more,

Henry's Fork Hatch Chart (Harriman Section)

MAYFLIES	TIMES	NOTES
Pale Morning Dun *(Ephemerella inermis)*	late June to early August	hatches mid-morning to mid-afternoon & spinner falls evening or morning; size 14-18
Blue-winged Olives (*Baetis* sp.)	June to early July mid-August to October	afternoon, especially during cloudy weather; size 20-22 typically afternoon, sometimes morning; size 18-22
Tiny Western Olive	August to September	late afternoon; size 24
Green Drake **(*Drunella grandis*)**	mid- to late June	best at upper Harriman, especially on cloudy days; size 10
Small Green Drake (*Drunella flavilinea*)	July	late afternoon-evening; size 14. Often called "Flav" or "slate-winged olive"
Brown Drake **(*Ephemera simulans*)**	late June to early July	Lower end of Harriman; typically at dusk; size 10
Tricos (*Tricorythodes*)	August to mid-September	mid-morning hatches; spinner falls. size 18-22
Speckled-wing Dun (*Callibaetis*)	mid-July to September	late morning, late afternoon; size 14-16
Mahogany Dun (*Paraleptophlebia*)	September	midday hatches. size 16
OTHER HATCHES		
Brachycentrus and *Hydropsyche* caddis	June to September	hatches can be prolific; down-wing patterns and emerger patterns best; size 14-16
Misc. Caddis	June to September	localized hatches and ovipositing flights of a variety of caddis. Carry down-wing patterns and emerger patterns in olive, tan, and brown. size 14-22
Ants/beetles	June to September	some fish will feed extensively on terrestrials; other will take ant/beetle patterns during mayfly hatches. size 14-20
Hoppers	July to September	warm, windy days are best, especially near grassy banks

Riverside to Warm River

Below the Osborn Springs reach, the Henry's Fork begins to assume an entirely new character. After meandering quietly through Harriman Park and down towards the homes at Pinehaven, the river begins to pick up speed, changing gradually into a pocket water/riffle environment as it approaches Riverside Campground and then hurrying down to Hatchery Ford. Below Hatchery Ford, the river plunges into Cardiac Canyon, where Sheep Falls and Lower Sheep Falls, Upper Mesa Falls and Lower

Mesa Falls, and several other rough-water sections make the river non-navigable.

Because of the treacherous wading, climbing about and lack of access, the Cardiac Canyon reach is not heavily fished. Yet some nice trout reside here, waiting to reward adventurous, strong-wading fly anglers.

The top end of this section is flotable. Put-in at Riverside Campground and take-out at Hatchery Ford, but *do not float beyond Hatchery Ford* because the next landmark is Sheep Falls about two miles downstream. Incidentally, just about any kind of small boat can float from Osborn Bridge down to Osborn Springs or on down to Riverside Campground. The float down to the campground covers only about seven miles, but launch bright and early as the hatches are strong and the fishing can really get in the way of the floating. The four-mile float from Riverside down to Hatchery Ford takes you through a series of rapids, some of which you may want to scout before attempting.

Drive-in/walk-in access to the sections below Pinehaven is available via several Forest Service roads. On most you'll have to park at the end and walk a short distance to the river. From the east bank, off Mesa Falls Scenic Route (47), the first access below Osborn Springs is the west extension of Hatchery Butte Road (this road also leads east to the headwaters region of the Warm River). Another spur leads toward the river about 2 1/2 miles further south and the next road takes you down to the Hatchery Ford area. The last spur before Mesa Falls leads over to Sheep Falls. You will find overlooks for the Mesa Falls and then the river flows past the old Bear Gulch Ski Area, where my Mom broke her leg one day during the early 70s. After cascading past Bear Gulch, the river swings to the southwest and picks up the Warm River at Stone Bridge.

From the Highway 20 side of the river (the west side) you can access Riverside Campground (which accepts and often requires reservations during the peak of summer). Just watch for the signs north of Little Butte Road; if you reach Swan Lake, you've gone too far. About four miles south of Riverside Campground, two spurs (FR 156 and FR 351) lead back to Hatchery Ford. Two miles south from there, you will find a spur (FR 163—Sheep Falls Road) leading over to Sheep Falls. Forest Service Road 164, another two miles south off Hwy. 20, leads through Anderson Mill Canyon down to the rim above Cardiac Canyon and Mesa Falls, but use Route 47 instead.

The fishing between Upper and Lower Mesa falls can be excellent and lonely: You have to climb down a steep trail that takes off from near the overlook. Study the water from the overlook first so you know what you're getting into. Then be careful with the rough, and at times treacherous, wading. Big dry-flies, nymphs and streamers are all productive here and an occasional 20-inch rainbow will provide ample excitement.

Below Grandview Campground, as the river plummets full-steam through the Bear Gulch reach, you can find great dry-fly fishing for small- and medium-sized trout, assuming you are willing to make the hike down into the canyon. An occasional monster of five or six pounds will reward persistent nymph or streamer anglers. A little spur road just past Grandview Campground provides access to the rim above the river or you can park along Route 47 in a couple spots and bushwhack it over to the canyon. You can also float this section given three minimum requirements: 1. A willingness and ability to slide a boat down the mountainside to get to the river; 2. The experience and ability to handle your boat through treacherous water and to negotiate Surprise Falls (about halfway down); 3. A fundamental lack of common sense and at least a temporary loss of sanity.

Throughout, the Cardiac Canyon reach of the Henry's Fork offers solitude and good fishing. The stonefly season between June and early July is best because the trout will smash big dry-flies with reckless abandon. When the salmonflies and golden stones are on the water, even the big rainbows will come to the surface, so fish of several pounds are not uncommon. In a few places, hopper season can offer good dry-fly action and some tremendous caddis hatches occur during the summer. Autumn is one of my favorite times here because other anglers are few and far between and the rainbows will devour streamer patterns.

A large evening hatch can make a fly angler wary of where to place his next cast.

Warm River to Ashton

At Stone Bridge, the Warm River joins the Henry's Fork as the latter swings to the west and flows around the south slope of the Island Park Caldera. In this easily flotable 10-odd-mile reach, the gradient lessens and the river slows from the grueling pace of Cardiac Canyon. Fishing can be good in this section—primarily from a boat— for cutt-bows, rainbows, cutthroat and brown trout, some of which reach impressive sizes.

River Road runs along the north bank (cross Stone Bridge) between the Warm River confluence and Ashton Reservoir (west of Hwy. 20), providing good access and several unimproved take-outs. The drift down from Warm River takes you under the highway bridge at the base of Ashton Hill and then a short distance down to the take-out at the top of Ashton Reservoir.

Stonefly hatches attract attention to this part of the river during early summer, with the salmonflies typically appearing between mid- and late May. Golden stones follow in June. Hopper patterns produce later in the year. Strong caddis and mayfly hatches offer good dry-fly opportunities as well. Pale morning duns (*Ephemerella*) and blue-winged olives (*Baetis*) are common and the gray drake (*Siphlonurus*) hatch that is so strong between Ashton and Chester makes a minor appearance here as well. Green drakes emerge during early or mid-June.

Ashton to Chester Backwaters

Chester Dam is a small diversion dam on the Henry's Fork just below the confluence with Fall River. The backwaters created by the dam hold some large rainbow trout and can be fished by float tube or small boat. If you choose the former, be aware that ample current runs through the backwaters and if you're not careful you might end up dangerously close to the diversion dam, where a thin but quick layer of water spills over the cement. The launch is on the east bank above the dam.

The stretch between Ashton Dam and Chester Backwaters offers some of the river's most unheralded fishing, especially during spring and again between midsummer and late autumn. The five-mile reach from Vernon Bridge down to Chester is a popular drift or you can add a couple miles by putting-in below Ora Bridge, a short distance down from Ashton Dam. To reach Ora Bridge, turn west at the main intersection in Ashton and drive about three miles to the river. The put-in is located on the east bank just below the bridge. The road to Vernon (Fritz) Bridge is located a mile south of Ashton on the fish hatchery road. Turn west at the signs leading to the hatchery (this is the west extension of Flagg Ranch Road).

This reach of the Henry's Fork is open all year and offers some good spring and late fall fishing along with the more traditional summer through early autumn opportunities. Hatches can be very strong and include green drakes, blue-winged olives and gray drakes, the latter of which comes off in strong numbers during summer. Some tremendous

caddis hatches occur during spring and summer, and the giant stoneflies appear during May, followed by golden stones during June and early July.

To find Chester Dam, follow Hwy. 20 to the town of Chester, just northeast of St. Anthony and southwest of Ashton. Exit at Chester and follow the sportsman's access signs to the diversion dam. Some rough camping is available—very rough if the local kids still use this place as a weekend beer garden.

Henry's Lake

For several decades eastern Idaho's Henry's Lake has been among the West's most popular still-water fly angling destinations. This super-fertile lake, located on the north edge of famed Island Park, offers fast-growing cutthroat-rainbow hybrids produced by the on-site state hatchery, along with Yellowstone cutthroat and some healthy-sized brook trout.

Beginning in 1976, the Idaho Department of Fish & Game began managing Henry's Lake as a trophy trout fishery. The results have been well-documented: Trout of 16 to 24 inches are common and fish up to eight pounds (sometimes larger still) are available. The brook trout and the rainbows that hybridized with the lake's native Yellowstone cutthroat are thought to have been introduced accidentally or at least unofficially. Both are exceptional game fish, so the IDFG manages for all three trout, including the two non-natives.

Cutthroat and hybrids make up the majority of the catch, making the occasional large brook trout a pleasant surprise. During the fall, however, fly anglers pursue the big brook trout with more success as the fish approach their spawning season.

Float-tubing has long been a popular method of fishing Henry's Lake.

Forrest Maxwell with a nice Henry's Lake cutthroat taken at Staley Springs.

Henry's Lake is shallow, averaging about 12 feet in depth. Its maximum depth is less than 30 feet and the lake covers more than 6,000 acres during a normal-water year. Henry's is also spring-fed and its most famous destination is the area around Staley Springs on the lake's northwest edge. The springs pump cool water into the lake during the warm, weed-laden summer months. Trout congregate at these springs, as do float tubers and boaters.

Late May through late July and mid-September through October generally offer the best fishing on Henry's Lake. The lake's biggest attraction is the early July damsel emergence. Henry's is loaded with trout foods and the damsels are nothing short of abundant. The mid-morning nymphal migration causes trout to feed in binges. Some days the adult damsel fishing can be productive and exciting.

In addition to the damsels, Henry's Lake trout feed heavily on scuds, leeches, *Callibaetis* mayfly nymphs and all manner of other still-water food items. Scud patterns should be light green, olive-tan or gray-green. A number of leech patterns will prove effective, although my favorite to this day is the Henry's Lake Leech: During the late 1970s, when he opened his fly shop (All Seasons Angler) in Pocatello, Jimmy Gabettas tied lots of flies and occasionally filled orders for fly anglers in the employ of The Loyd Company—a real estate appraisal company owned by my uncle and employing my father, my cousin Gary and a handful of other fly anglers who reveled in doing their appraisal work in the Island Park country.

Among other patterns, Jimmy sold them Henry's Lake Leeches, simple Woolly Bugger-like flies that featured a medium brown marabou tail and a body of brown-olive variegated chenille. The brown saddle hackle was clipped short and the hook (typically a size 6 or 8, 3XL) was bent up at an angle.

Leech and scud patterns produce throughout the season on Henry's Lake and by fall, streamer patterns can entice large brook trout, which congregate in the vicinity of tributary creeks.

Despite its potential for large numbers of big trout, Henry's Lake is not without its problems. The low-water years of the late 80s and early 90s were especially hard on the brook trout, which could not utilize some of their traditional spawning streams. The lake is so rich that plant growth can become a significant problem, especially during low-water years. The big winter-kill of 1991 was a direct result of a tremendous algae bloom coupled with low water—a condition that left little oxygen available to the trout after ice-up.

To combat this problem, IDFG now uses large aerators to increase the water's oxygen content during winter. Through it all, however, Henry's Lake remains the crown jewel in Idaho's still-water fisheries program.

Henry's Lake offers eight access points, four of which require a fee as they are on private land.

These fee-access areas are as follows:

1. Henry's Lake State Park at the outlet on the lake's southeast shore. Follow Highway 20 north, crossing Henry's Lake Outlet. About two miles past the outlet, look for signs and a left-hand turn leading to the state park.

2. Henry's Lake Lodge. Follow Hwy. 20 north past the turnoff to the state park. Veer left (northwest) on Hwy. 287 and cross Targhee Creek. Follow the signs and take a left-hand turn to the lodge.

3. Wild Rose Ranch. Follow Hwy. 287 past the turnoff to the lodge and along the lake's north shore. After crossing Wild Rose Creek, watch for signs leading a short distance down to Wild Rose.

4. Staley Springs Resort. Drive past the turnoff to Wild Rose Ranch a short distance to Forest Service Road 055. Turn left (south) and drive less than a mile to Staley Springs Resort.

The no-fee access areas are as follows:

1. State Hatchery. Follow Hwy. 287 along the north shore and watch for the signs (east of Wild Rose Ranch).

2. Frome County Park. Just past (south of) Staley Springs on FR 055. (A fairly short float-tube paddle from the county park takes you to Staley Springs in front of the resort.)

3. The Cliffs (Hope Creek) and Henry's Lake Outlet. Before crossing the Outlet on Hwy. 20 southeast of the lake, turn left on FR 053 (Red Rock Lakes Road). A few miles down FR053, a dirt road turns off to the right and leads to the outlet. The next turn-off to the north leads to the launch at the Cliffs.

Henry's Lake is a big lake and one that sits at high elevation (6596 feet). Summer thunderstorms are common and can arrive with scant warning during the afternoon, even after a perfect morning. High winds—or at least incessant ones—can be a fact of life, especially during the afternoon.

Island Park Reservoir

An 8,400-acre impoundment at full pool, Island Park Reservoir, whose outflow feeds Box Canyon, traditionally offers good fall fishing for big rainbows. An irrigation storage, the reservoir's water level fluctuates dramatically. When full or close to full during the summer, the reservoir is primarily the domain of kokanee trollers. During fall, however, the reservoir is drawn down and the trout feed ravenously in preparation for winter.

October is the best month to fish the myriad bays, coves, points, and channels for rainbows that will average two to four pounds and sometimes reach six to ten pounds. The reservoir is open all year and those willing to brave the last fishable days of late October through mid- to late November are often rewarded with big, bright rainbows and few other people.

West End Campground provides the best access. Take Green Canyon Road, which departs Hwy. 20 just south of Osborn Bridge. Follow the signs to West End Campground. A number of spur roads lead to different coves and points (beware of shoreline mud at low water). A float tube or pontoon boat will suffice. If you're fishing by boat, you've got lots of options, but consider running north to the mouths of Sheridan and Icehouse creeks.

Any number of wet-flies will do the trick when the trout are on the feed during fall. You can't go wrong with a black, brown or olive leech pattern. Other effective patterns include Carey Specials, streamers of various kinds, scuds and Zug Bugs. Those who venture to the reservoir during summer, beginning around mid-June, might encounter damsel and *Callibaetis* mayfly hatches; Chironomids stir surface activity on still mornings, otherwise fish leeches, scuds and damsel nymphs.

South Fork Snake

Not all that long ago, out-of-state fly anglers heading for Idaho made a beeline for the Henry's Fork, Henry's Lake and Silver Creek. Things have changed. Super-productive waters like the South Fork of the Boise, the St. Joe and Kelly Creek—once well-kept secrets by the Idaho fly-fishing community—have become destination waters in their own right. No river in the state has experienced the transition from local favorite to national destination like the South Fork of Snake River in eastern Idaho.

The South Fork that we know as a trout fishery begins at Palisades Dam, where the Snake River that originates across the border in Wyoming is finally tethered in the form of 16,000-acre Palisades Reservoir. The river then flows northwesterly towards its confluence with the Henry's Fork north of Idaho Falls. Highway 26 out of Idaho Falls follows the river along most of its course.

The South Fork is home to populations of wild cutthroat and brown trout, along with some rainbows, cutt-bows and lots of whitefish. Cutthroat over 14 inches are common and fish to 20 inches are available. The brown trout, which are fewer in number, can grow larger still, with specimens of 14 to 24 inches hardly raising eyebrows among regulars on the river.

The cutthroat—Snake River finespots and Yellowstone cutts—dominate the upper and middle reaches of this 64-mile-long tailwater fishery. As you progress down river, however, brown trout become more numerous. In the lower 10 or 12 miles, brown trout outnumber cutthroat. Rainbow trout are not common, but their mere presence leads to the inevitable hybridizing with the wild cutthroat, a mix that produces the "cut-bows" found in many waters where both species exist. The IDFG is grappling with this potential problem.

That the South Fork's trout grow as big as they do is testament to the river's fertility more so than to the fact that the stream is a tailwater fishery. Palisades Dam, however, does play a critical role in the fishing opportunity each season: During late spring and summer, irrigators on the Snake River Plain need water and they get it in part through a series of canals that drink from the South Fork. To meet the water needs, Palisades Dam is uncorked, causing high water levels through the summer. Not until Labor Day or so are the releases curtailed. During summer, when the major hatches occur, South Fork anglers contend with high flows that make floating easy, but wading difficult.

The hatches on the South Fork are less than predictable in their timing each year. Everything depends on the water load in Palisades Reservoir during snow-melt. Heavy snow years mean big releases and high, cold water. Hatches start a little later than they will after lean winters. Nonetheless, the South Fork offers a procession of exceptional hatches, with stoneflies, caddis and mayflies all well represented.

Also, the water temperature varies considerably between the upper river and the lower river. Releases from Palisades Dam cool the upper river, but by the time you reach the lower-gradient agricultural area between Lorenzo and Menan Buttes (near the confluence with the Henry's Fork), temperatures are typically at least five or six degrees warmer.

The stonefly carnival on the South Fork rivals that of any other Western river: Hordes of anglers descend on the river to enjoy explosive rises to big dry-flies. Golden stoneflies and salmonflies begin to emerge during late June below Heise and the hatch progresses upriver steadily, reaching the canyon within a week or so and reaching Swan Valley a week or so after that.

The golden stones outlast the giant salmonflies, but trout remember the latter for a week or more after the emergence ends. Beware the pale

A large brown trout.

GREG THOMAS

Fall Creek Falls on the South Fork Snake.

morning dun (*Ephemerella*) mayfly hatches that can steal the show on a localized basis, especially in places where trout have been pounded by stonefly patterns. Likewise, an unusual but sumptuous treat during stonefly time is the occasional fishable hatch of green drakes (*Drunella grandis*).

The PMDs, along with *Baetis* (blue-winged olive) mayflies, comprise the most significant mayfly hatches on the South Fork. Both hatch best on overcast days and during rainy weather. Look for *Baetis* just about any time, but especially early and late in the season. PMDs hatch during the summer and hot weather will compress their emergence and spinner falls toward morning and evening.

Many other mayfly genera are represented in the South Fork, but not all produce widespread, dense hatches. During the summer, you might encounter hatches of pale evening duns (Light Cahills) of the genera *Stenonema* and *Heptagenia*, depending on where you are fishing. Pink Alberts (*Epeorus albertae*) make an appearance around midsummer and mahogany duns (*Paraleptophlebia*) hatch during September.

Caddis emergences can be nothing short of staggering at times and an emergence of one kind or another is a nightly occurrence during the summer. Rarely do you need to worry about particular genera—just be ready with emerging pupa patterns (e.g. X-Caddis), down-wing patterns (e.g. Spent Partridge Caddis, Quad-wing Caddis) and adult patterns like the ever-functional Elk Hair Caddis. *Brachycentrus* and *Hydropsyche* caddis are abundant, but so too are many other types. Even October caddis (*Dicosmoecus*), the giant orange sedge, make an autumn appearance.

During any decent hatch of mayflies or caddisflies, South Fork trout can get down right selective. A size 4 Stimulator on a 3X tippet might deliver rise after rise during the stonefly hatch, but the same fish that seemed so gullible then can be frustratingly selective when an evening hatch of caddis erupts on a quiet tailout, or when a dense hatch of PMDs gathers cutthroat into gulping pods. Be prepared to fish a long, light

tippet on a very gentle delivery. The same downstream presentations that you might employ up at Harriman on the Henry's Fork will prove equally effective on the freestone waters of the South Fork

While the golden stones and salmonflies provide the best stonefly hatches, other stonefly species are common on the South Fork as well. Most prevalent are the brown willow flies (a type of golden stonefly) and the attractive little Yellow Sallies (*Isoperla*), which hatch sporadically during July and August.

By mid-July, hopper season begins and by August a hopper cast tight against brushy banks will hearken you back to the stonefly days of a few weeks prior. Hoppers remain effective all the way through September in most years and often into October.

If you're serious about the South Fork's big brown trout, concentrate your efforts on the lower end of the river. Decent browns will take stoneflies and hoppers on the surface, but the real hogs are highly predatory on other fish, including the river's abundant supply of sculpins. These fish are best duped with big, heavy streamers like sculpin patterns, Woolly Buggers, Muddlers and Zonkers. A floating line will work with heavily weighted streamers, but a high-density sink-tip is more useful, especially in deeper water. Brown trout migrate upriver during October and November to seek spawning gravel, so some anglers fish the runs below Palisades Dam until the end of the season.

Even if the fishing is a little off, a float down the South Fork takes you through some beautiful country. Game is everywhere: Deer are common and elk, especially during autumn, are abundant. Moose often graze the backwaters and adjacent meadows. The South Fork supports one of the most productive populations of nesting bald eagles in the Rocky Mountains. A handful of peregrine falcon pairs nest in the canyon as well. Many other birds nest or winter on or near the river as well: goshawks, great horned owls, osprey, ruffed grouse, herons, sandhill cranes and more than 100 others.

South Fork Access

On the whole, the South Fork is best accessed by boat, with drift boats being the odds-on favorite among fly anglers. The river offers numerous boat accesses. Walking/wading anglers need not despair: Foot access is better than it might appear assuming you are willing to use your feet and to ferret out some of the more remote access areas.

The first 13 miles, from Palisades Dam down to Swan Valley Bridge and Spring Creek Boat Ramp, offer several access sites for wading anglers. The stretch below the dam offers lots of cutthroat (and no shortage of whitefish) and they are especially reachable during the low-water period of September and October.

In fact, autumn is by far the best time for wading anglers because the low water allows access to countless places that are unwadeable during summer. If your not into the float scene, visit the South Fork during September or October and plan to do some walking, brush-busting and bank-scrambling to reach areas that haven't been heavily fished.

Highway 26 roughly parallels the north bank between Palisades Dam and Spring Creek, but an abundance of private property limits access on that side. Palisades Creek sportsman's access/Irwin Boat Access, 3 1/2 miles downstream from the dam, covers 15 acres and offers good river access, camping, outhouses and a cement ramp.

The Irwin to Spring Creek drift covers an easy nine miles and is a good choice for covering the productive braids of the Swan Valley reach. You can also put-in back up at Palisades Dam (there is quite a bit of camping space here as well).

This upper section of the river actually has fairly good walk-in access from the south bank, which is bordered by ample acreage of Forest Service land. Forest Service Road 058 (Snake River Road) follows the river all the way from Palisades Dam to Swan Valley Bridge. The down-river turnoff is just off the southeast corner of the bridge (at the Spring Creek Boat Ramp); the upstream access is across Palisades Dam.

Below Swan Valley Bridge, foot-access opportunities are limited on the highway side of the river. The 17-acre Conant Access (with its recently re-designed ramp) is heavily used by floaters, but does offer access to some decent wade fishing during fall. Spring Creek to Conant is a simple two-mile drift; for a longer day, put-in farther upriver.

Below Conant, the South Fork enters a steep, rather remote canyon. Floaters often run from Conant, through the canyon, and down to Byington Park Access, with overnight trips being best if you want lots of fishing time. Foot traffic in the canyon is restricted in some areas during the summer to protect nesting bald eagles, falcons, and herons. These sites are posted with orange signs.

Overnighters between Conant and Lufkin Bottom (upstream from Byington) must complete a self-issue permit (available at the put-ins) and must use one of the 15 designated camp areas. These designated areas range from two to 40 acres in size and offer a variety of possible campsites. They are marked with big white signs. Also, any overnighters in this reach must carry and use a portable toilet.

The Conant to Byington float covers 25 beautiful miles. Both ends feature excellent cement ramps. You can reduce the distance by taking-out or putting-in at Cottonwood Access (camping, cement ramp, bathrooms) or Wolf Flat (no facilities, bank launch). The Conant to Cottonwood drift covers 14 miles; Wolf Flat is seven miles below Cottonwood. Both these sites are located on the north bank and are accessed via the Kelly Canyon Road east of Heise.

To reach these sites, follow Hwy. 26 to 160th and turn north toward the river. Drive two miles, straight through the intersection with Old Ririe Highway, and veer right at Heise Road. Cross Heise Bridge and turn right, heading east for 2.4 miles to the intersection of roads 206 and 218. Turn left and follow 218 (Kelly Canyon Road) around Kelly Mountain.

The South Fork of the Snake is a classic drifter's river; here, two anglers fish an October afternoon,
a time when the water runs low and clear.

Playing a trout on the South Fork.

Continue straight at the 217/218 intersection near Lookout Mountain (you are now on 217) and follow the road down to the river. Turn left (upstream) to reach Cottonwood; turn right to reach Wolf Flat.

Road 206 gets you there as well, but over some rough gravel as you skirt the river's north bank (although it is only a few miles to Wolf Flat from here). Bank access is good along this section of the north bank, with Forest Service land predominating. The road leaves the river near Lufkin Bottom above Cottonwood, but a pack trail continues upstream.

Kelly Island Campground is located on FR 206 just past the 206/218 intersection. This campground, which is directly across from Byington, offers some good bank access. Additional foot access is available west of Heise Bridge along the north bank; park at the canal diversion and walk downriver.

Conant Boat Ramp, incidentally, is just off the highway in Conant Valley a couple miles northwest of Swan Valley Bridge. The site is well marked and lies adjacent to South Fork Lodge and Fly Shop. Byington Access ("Poplar") is well off the highway: Turn north off Hwy. 26 at 175th East and drive two miles to 143rd North. Turn east and drive a mile to the park.

Byington is a good put-in for floating the lower river and some good wade/bank fishing is available from the canal access road immediately east of the park. Drive through the parking lot and onto a rough gravel road which runs between the river and the canal for half a mile. The canal itself sometimes holds some nice trout.

The 24 miles of river below Byington offers four take-outs, the best two being the bank launch at Lorenzo Access near Hwy. 20 and the cement ramp at Menan Bridge west of Hwy. 20 and below the confluence with the Henry's Fork. Byington to Lorenzo covers 15 miles and is a day's float if you stop to fish quite a bit.

The other two take-outs offer shorter floats, but they can prove difficult to use: Heise (three miles below Byington) is a bank launch that requires considerable labor and Twin Bridges (seven miles below Byington) is a high-water-only ramp. Lorenzo is the prudent choice.

While the South Fork offers straight-forward floating with no severe rapids, there are several serious hazards of which you must be aware. Several water diversion structures are located between Byington and the Henry's Fork confluence. Steer clear of these. Among the most dangerous is the Dry Beds Canal diversion 1.5 miles below Byington, which is extremely hazardous. Stay well to the north bank here as the headgate for the diversion lies along the south bank and it sucks in nearly half the river. Three miles below Twin Bridges is the Reid Canal diversion on the north bank.

The lower end of the river, below Twin Bridges, is comprised of braided channels and lots of cottonwood snags that end up as log jams and sweepers in the river. Local floaters sometimes refer to the log jams below Twin Bridges as "the Snags." In part because of the difficulty in navigating through the stumps, driftwood jams, and side channels, this lower end of the river is not nearly as popular with floaters as the upper and middle portions.

South Fork Fly Patterns

Naturally, every South Fork regular has his or her favorite fly patterns, be they hatch-matching flies or attractor types. The list below includes many of the long-standing favorite patterns along with some popular newcomers. See fly plates and selected dressings for further description. Numerous fly patterns can be used interchangeably for the major South Fork hatches. During the salmonfly hatch, for example, old standbys like the Sofa Pillow, Improved Sofa Pillow, Bird's Stone and Stimulator will fish as well as the countless contemporary patterns. Just choose your weapon and concentrate on presentation.

Stonefly Dries
Lawson's Henry's Fork Stonefly
 (Bullet Head Stonefly)
Foam Head Stone
Marcella Trout Fly
Improved Sofa Pillow
Bird's Stone
Lawson's Yellow Sally
Little Yellow Sally
Mormon Girl

Caddis Dries
Elk Hair Caddis
Spent Partridge Caddis
Deer Hair Caddis
X-Caddis
Bucktail Caddis

Attractor Dries
Royal Humpy
Royal Wulff
H & L Variant
Royal Trude
Renegade
Super Renegade
Chernobyl Ant
Double Humpy
Turck's Tarantula

Terrestrial/Midge Dries
Griffith's Gnat
Dave's Hopper
Bullet Head Hopper
Crystal Ant

Mayfly Dries
Red Quill
Pink CDC Emerger
Pink Cahill
Pink Cahill Parachute
Pink Cahill Compara-dun
Pink Cahill CDC Dun
PMD CDC Dun
PMD Sparkle Dun
Lawson's CDC PMD Emerger
Parachute *Baetis*
Baetis Floating Nymph

Wet Flies/Nymphs
Beadhead Prince
Beadhead Pheasant Tail Nymph
Beadhead Hare's Ear Nymph
Brassy
Bitch Creek
George's Brown Stone
Orange & Black Stonefly Nymph
Box Canyon Stone
Peeking Caddis
Super Renegade
Super X
Fizzle
Mormon Girl (wet)
Olive Bead Head

Streamers
Zonker
Double Bunny
Falls River Flasher
Kiwi Muddler
Whitlock Sculpin
Woolly Bugger
Beadhead Woolly Bugger

South Fork Tributaries

Several tributary streams to the South Fork offer good summer/fall fishing for cutthroat. Pine Creek flows southwest from the Big Hole Mountains, entering the river below Conant. State Route 31 follows Pine Creek from Swan Valley into the mountains and then continues over to Teton Basin. A late opener (July 1) protects spawning cutthroat (including some surprisingly big fish) in Pine Creek and its tributaries. Some of these fish stick around for the balance of the summer, working their way back downriver as autumn approaches.

Burns Creek opens even later (Sept. 1) for the same reason, but its autumn fishing can be very good. Burns Creek joins the South Fork near Cottonwood Access on the north bank.

Palisades Creek originates in the Big Hole as well, entering the South Fork about three miles downstream from Palisades Dam. The creek offers some decent fishing, but better still are Upper and Lower Palisades lakes. Both are accessible by good Forest Service trails leaving Palisades Creek

Campground. A four-mile hike takes you to diminutive Lower Palisades Lake, where cutthroat up to 13 inches are common and fish up to 18 inches are not unusual. Continue past Lower Palisades Lake some two miles until you reach trail size 099, which crosses the creek and heads about 2/3 of a mile to Upper Palisades Lake. The upper lake, though much larger, holds lots of smallish cutthroat. Strong *Callibaetis* mayfly hatches occur on both lakes during summer, but autumn finds substantially fewer folks on the trail.

Fall Creek joins the South Fork in dramatic style just upstream from Swan Valley Bridge on the south bank: The creek spills out onto a travertine outcropping and plunges over 60-foot Fall Creek Falls. You can visit the falls by driving a short distance up Snake River Road (FR 058). The creek itself is fishable for quite a few miles along FR 077.

McCoy Creek and Bear Creek enter the south shore of Palisades Reservoir. Consult the Targhee National Forest Map (Palisades Ranger District) and Caribou National Forest Map (Soda Springs Ranger District) for directions. Big Elk Creek originates in Wyoming, but its lower five miles flow through Idaho and into a narrow arm on the northwest side of Palisades Reservoir.

The Teton Range forms a splendid backdrop for anglers fishing the Teton River in the valley section.

Palisades Reservoir

Though hardly a destination water in a place where its modest offerings must compete with a world-class river, Palisades Reservoir nonetheless offers some good float-tube fishing for resident cutthroat and brown trout, the latter averaging about 16 inches. Float-tubers can fish the narrow bays, especially where ramps or gentle slopes allow for easy access. Otherwise, steep shoreline margins make access difficult in many places. Autumn is best, especially October. Concentrate on the bays with major tributaries such as McCoy Creek and Big Elk Creek. A number of boat ramps are scattered about on this 16,000-acre reservoir (whose level fluctuates regularly). Hwy. 26 follows the South Fork Snake east out of Idaho Falls and eventually traces the reservoir's northeast shoreline.

Teton River, Valley Stretch

If ever there existed an idyllic setting for a first-rate trout stream, the Teton River has to occupy that place. The Teton emanates from a convergence of mountain streams and small spring creeks in the Teton Basin west by northwest of Idaho Falls. The entire region lies within the shadow of the spectacular Teton Range whose jagged peaks dominate the eastern horizon.

For its first 30 miles the Teton meanders through the pastoral farmlands of the Teton Basin, once home to the famed trapper's rendezvous at "Pierre's Hole." Picking up spring feeds and small tributaries along its winding course, this upper section of the river is often referred to as the "valley stretch." Most of the upper river is shallow, but its deeper pools, channels and overhanging banks provide ample habitat for native Yellowstone cutthroat, wild rainbows and brook trout, and the rainbow-cutthroat hybrids that are invariably present where hatchery programs have been superimposed on wild cutthroat populations.

This entire valley reach offers all the qualities of a spring creek experience: Slow, flat water, excellent hatches and selective trout that occasionally reach 20 inches. Cutthroat, brook trout and hybrids of eight to 14 inches are the norm.

Spring run-off ravages the river until sometime between late June and mid-July, depending on snowpack. When flows stabilize, the dry-fly action begins. Caddis and mayflies predominate. A hatch of Western green drakes begins about the time run-off subsides. The drakes can provide exceptional dry-fly action, especially on overcast days, but the hatch lasts only a week or two. Localized blue-winged olive hatches begin early, but their regularity seems to be weather dependent. Overcast days can trigger dense hatches of these tiny mayflies. Dependable pale morning dun hatches begin as water levels stabilize after run-off and continue through the summer. Day in and day out, PMDs provide the top summer mayfly action on the valley stretch.

Late summer brings renewed blue-winged olive activity as well as localized speckled-wing dun (*Callibaetis*) emergences. Tricos appear mid-morning (and sometimes in lesser densities during the late evening). Gray drakes, the only large mayfly of autumn begin to appear mid- to late August. The hatches can be fairly heavy but they tend to be localized.

Myriad caddis inhabit the Teton River, but I've certainly never bothered trying to key them out and I'm not sure one needs to do so. Carry emerger patterns (e.g. X-Caddis) and down-wing patterns like the Spent Partridge Caddis or Quad-wing Caddis in sizes 14-18. I've seen dense flights of little black caddis during late summer, but I've not seen trout get too excited about them.

Some of my most memorable Teton River days date back to my formative years when dad was doing appraisal work in the valley one August. I tagged along a few times and carried nothing more than hopper patterns, which drew explosive rises when tossed against the grassy banks. To this day, hopper season is one of the river's prime attractions, with August and September being best.

Access to the river in the Teton Valley can be a little confusing, especially because many area roads are marked with numbers rather than the names shown on maps. Floaters can put-in at any of several ramps and fish waters not readily accessible to bank anglers. The river flows almost entirely through private property, so bank access is quite limited. A knock on a door can still get you to the river, however, so don't be afraid to ask permission. The lack of public land and the meandering nature of this small river creates an ideal opportunity for floaters. Just about any kind of small craft can make the journey, with canoes and small prams being ideal.

You can reach the Teton Valley on Hwy. 33, which joins Hwy. 20 between St. Anthony and Rexburg or by hopping over the Big Hole Mountains along Pine Creek Road from the South Fork of the Snake at Swan Valley. Both routes are quick and painless. If you are coming from the east, Hwy. 33 climbs over Victor Pass from Jackson Hole, Wyoming and leads directly to the head of the valley at Victor.

Once you reach the valley, the best bank access is at Rainey sportsman's access, a 1,600-acre rec. site that includes ample room for camping and some very productive stretches of river for those willing to walk and wade. To reach Rainey, follow Hwy. 33 about four miles past the little town of Tetonia (heading south) and watch for the sportsman's access sign at Cache (Packsaddle) Road. Follow this road about five miles to Cache Bridge (which offers a good boat launch). Drive over the bridge and then take the next left. Follow a bumpy gravel road about 2.5 miles to Rainey.

The uppermost public boat ramp is at White Bridge on North Cedron Road which turns west off Hwy. 33 about 2 1/2 miles north of Victor. Teton Creek sportsman's access at the Bates Road Bridge is the next access downstream. Look for the sportsman's access sign on Hwy. 33 about two miles south of Driggs, then follow the gravel road west some three miles to the bridge. Float distance is about five miles between White Bridge and Bates Bridge. The next ramp downstream is located at Buxton Bridge, about four miles further. Turn west at the main intersection in Driggs and follow this paved road until you reach the river. In Driggs, this road is signed as Little Road, but maps will show its westerly extension as Buxton Road. An impressive heron rookery used to grace a stand of cottonwoods to the south of Buxton Road, east of the river. I don't know if the rookery is still active, but if so it is quite a sight during the nesting season.

Cache Bridge offers the next boat access as well as access to Rainey (which also offers a good cement ramp). The final ramp, at the lower end of the valley, is at Harrop's Bridge on Hwy. 33 four miles west of Tetonia. Don't float beyond this bridge unless you've had plenty of experience negotiating the ferocious currents of the Teton River Canyon below. The total float from White Bridge or Bates Bridge down to Hwy. 33 takes more than a day, so many floaters put-in at Rainey or Cache Bridge for shorter floats that allow for more fishing time. Or you can float any of the segments above Hwy. 33 and find good fishing.

In addition to the no-frills campground at Rainey, the area offers several National Forest campgrounds: Pine Creek along Pine Creek Road a few miles southwest of Victor, Harris and Trail Creek campgrounds along Hwy. 33 southeast of Victor, and Teton Canyon Campground east of Driggs. Lodging and supplies are available in the small towns of Driggs, Victor, and Tetonia.

Teton River, Canyon Section

In stark contrast to the placid, meandering waters of the upper Teton, the river's canyon reach is a rampaging, comparatively inaccessible, stretch of boulder-strewn white water and is home to the river's largest trout. A short distance below Harrop's Bridge, the Teton descends into a desert-like canyon whose volcanic rims make entry difficult and whose tumbling rapids challenge even the most experienced white-water kayakers. For some 15 miles from Hwy. 33 down to the Bitch Creek confluence, the river is essentially unfloatable and should be attempted only by the most experienced/insane white-water enthusiasts.

The cutthroat, rainbow and hybrids in this section average larger than their brethren upstream in the valley section and can exceed 20 inches. Stoneflies—salmonflies and goldens—provide the most anticipated action in the canyon and hoppers produce the top surface action later in the summer. Caddis hatches occur throughout the summer and streamer patterns can fool some very large trout.

Towards the lower end of the canyon section, one can visit the remnants of the river's greatest claim to fame, Teton Dam. By Saturday, June 5, 1976, a three-year construction project had resulted in a huge earth dam whose reservoir was filling for the first time. The new dam collapsed that day, sending a massive wall of water from the new reservoir plummeting through the canyon and out onto the Snake River Plain below. Small farm communities like Sugar City were decimated and it remains a minor miracle that only 11 people lost their lives. I lived with my family near Pocatello at that time and I'll never forget the radio broadcasts urging people to take refuge on the hill occupied by Rick's College in Rexburg.

That summer, after order was restored, we piled into the car to take a drive through the ravaged landscape. Entire houses, lifted off their foundations, stood in the middle of clean-swept fields. Long sections of pavement were picked up, moved a quarter mile, and set back down. Roofs, intact, lay upside down. A few big trees, stripped of all but their largest branches, stood like lone sentinels amidst the carnage. It was an economic disaster—and an environmental one from which the lower canyon has not fully recovered.

When you visit the Teton River country, take time to visit the old dam site. Follow Hwy. 33 east from Hwy. 20 until you see the signs for the site a few miles east of the little town of Newdale. Standing as a stark reminder is a huge pyramid of earth in the middle of the wide canyon—the only remnant of the dam itself. Across the canyon is an old cement spillway flume, arcing steeply toward the river below and painted in colorful graffiti. Downstream the scars from the disaster are apparent as a wide swath of sediment-laden cobble forces the river against the canyon wall.

Trout populations have recovered in the section of canyon affected by the flood, but the fishing will likely never be the same. What was once gravel-rich pocket water is now a series of meandering pools and fast chutes created when the canyon's sides collapsed into the river after being suddenly relieved of the water pressure from the newly formed reservoir. In Snake River Country: Flies and Waters, Bruce Staples writes, "A salmonid fishery remains and is improving; however, in the gutted canyon the Teton River will continue for decades to be only a remnant of what it once was."

Before the dam was built, the most popular access on the canyon section was at the Linderman Ranch. This site is no longer accessible, however, because the reservoir's sudden drawdown washed out part of the road.

Above the area trashed by the dam's collapse, the Teton remains much as it was, with healthy populations of trout that can grow to impressive sizes. Below Harrop Bridge, the first access to the canyon section is at Felt Dam. Follow Powerline Road west out of Felt off Hwy. 32 (Hwy. 32 turns north off Hwy. 33 about three miles east of Harrop's Bridge) until you reach the Felt Dam parking lot. Look for the unmarked trail below the gate and be prepared for a steep adventurous descent to the mouth of Badger Creek. A sportsman's access area along Powerline Road will also lead down to Badger Creek, which offers decent fishing as well.

Downstream of the Felt Dam access are two access areas with rough ramps (both of which were built for and intended for use by reservoir boaters before Teton Dam collapsed). The first, Spring Hollow, is some 6.5 miles below Felt Dam on the north bank. To find Spring Hollow, turn north off Hwy. 33 onto Hwy. 32 and drive just over 15 miles to a county road that turns off to the left just past France. From Ashton, drive through the little wide spot called Drummond and watch for the turnoff on your right approximately 3.5 miles further.

Bear in mind that the rapids within the old reservoir site require strong boating skills. Even experienced oarsmen should allow plenty of time for scouting the many drops.

The downstream ramp is located just upriver from the old dam site on the south bank. Follow Hwy. 33 through Newdale and watch for the signs leading to the dam site. The ramp is accessed via a rough gravel road to the right just about opposite the dam overlook parking area. After about a mile, turn left to the take-out. Four-wheel-drive vehicles can drive into the canyon on the next left turn, but you can walk it just as fast and with a lot less wear and tear. Float distance between the two ramps is about 15 miles. Foot access is available below the old dam site as well. Just walk down the gated gravel road just east of the overlook. Another access is a few miles downstream at Hog Hollow Bridge, where the river leaves the canyon.

From Warm Springs Campground, you can walk up the old railroad bed to reach the canyon section. Or you can drive to the top of the canyon and walk down the railroad grade or from Warm River Springs. Included in the adventure is a long tunnel through the mountainside. To reach the springs and the top of the canyon, follow Route 47 north over Warm River Bridge and head up the hill past Mesa Falls. Watch for Warm River Road on the right (FR 150). Follow FR 150 about three miles up to FR 154, which accesses the trail and Warm River Springs. You can also scramble down into the canyon from FR 367 (Wood Road #1), which turns north off Route 47, opposite Bear Gulch, as you swing up the hill on the way to Mesa Falls.

The Warm River's diminutive upper reaches are a real treat, especially if you're willing to choose a stretch away from the road and walk through the meadows and lodgepoles to get there. Small brook trout abound and though they lack for size, they are eager to pounce on dry-flies. Warm River Road roughly parallels the upper river for most of its length.

If you're coming from Island Park instead of Ashton, follow Route 47 (Mesa Falls Scenic Route) from Harriman Park down to the Warm River. You can cut over to the upper river on either Hatchery Butte Road or FR 112 (Eccles Road), both of which turn east off Route 47 near Osborn Springs. (Hatchery Butte Road, the quicker of the two routes, is a couple miles past Osborn Springs).

Fall River

Like a number of fine trout streams in eastern Idaho, the Fall (or Falls) River is overshadowed by famous neighbors such as the Henry's Fork and the South Fork. Nonetheless, it is a fine trout stream in its own right and anglers willing to do a little exploring and a little bushwhacking can find themselves alone on long sections of the Fall River.

Rainbows, along with a few cutthroats and hybrids, inhabit the Fall River, with fish to 14 inches being fairly common and a few to 20 inches or so being available in the stream's lower end. The Fall River's headwaters drain a corner of Yellowstone National Park before the river comes plummeting into Idaho just a couple miles below the park's southwest boundary. At this point, the river is flowing within the Targhee National Forest and is a typical mountain stream offering productive pocket water fishing in a scenic mountain canyon.

Primitive Forest Service roads offer approaches from only a couple places along Cave Falls Road north of the river and the old Flagg Ranch Road, which roughly parallels the south side of the canyon. Bushwhacking into the canyon from these roads or from along Flagg Ranch Road itself is a fairly simple proposition for the adventurous. About three river miles west of the Targhee National Forest's western boundary, the Fall River crosses under a bridge that offers access to the canyon. Property owners along the lower reaches of the river will usually grant permission for anglers to fish the river. Closer to Ashton, several other roads cross the river, including the bridge on Flagg Ranch Road southeast of Marysville.

The Fall River is rich in caddis and stoneflies, offering the late June hatches of large stoneflies common to all the region's freestone rivers. Late summer brings hopper fishing.

Warm River

The Warm River gathers it cold, clean waters from major springs and from mountain streams that drain the border country of Idaho and Wyoming on the eastern edge of Island Park. The river flows north to south before plunging into a canyon and swinging southwest to join the Henry's Fork east of Ashton.

The best fishing on this small river is found in the riffles and pocket waters of the canyon below Warm River Springs. Here rainbows thrive, along with an occasional brookie and cutthroat. As you approach the lower end of the river, small brown trout become more and more common along with hatchery-reared rainbows. In the canyon, wild rainbows of nine to 13 inches are common and fish to 16 inches are available. Caddis hatches predominate, but stoneflies hatch in the canyon section during early and midsummer.

Spring water.

Robinson Creek

If you're looking for secluded, small-stream fishing in a remote setting, try Robinson Creek Canyon where rainbows, cutthroat, brook trout and brown trout provide lots of action. Most will average pan-sized, but 14- to 18-inch fish are not uncommon in the more distant reaches.

Access to the upper stretches of Robinson Creek is via the Cave Falls Road south of Warm River. You can climb down a trail at Horseshoe Lake, just outside the Yellowstone National Park Boundary, or you can take Forest Service Road 470 (Sawmill Creek), park at its end, and walk into the canyon. FR 470 turns north off Cave Falls Road about a mile before you reach Horseshoe Lake Road (FR 246).

Further downstream, FR 241 crosses the creek, providing good access to the lower reaches on private property. FR 241 turns off Cave Falls Road 4 1/2 miles east of Hwy. 47, or you can approach from the north off Fish Creek Road. You can also hike into the canyon from several closed spur roads off FR 092 (which turns right off Fish Creek Road east of the FR 241 turnoff).

Robinson Creek offers good early summer stonefly hatches and strong caddis hatches throughout the summer. Hoppers appear midsummer and the August/September fishing can be very good with hopper patterns.

Small Creeks and Lakes in Targhee National Forest

When I was a kid growing up in St. Anthony, I had ample opportunity to practice fly angling on the small streams in Island Park. Later, when I started making annual autumn grouse hunting trips to the Centennial Range to the northwest, I stumbled on some fun small-stream fishing on the drainages above Kilgore.

In the former group, are waters like Rock Creek and Fish Creek, both tributaries to Robinson Creek. Partridge Creek, a tributary to the upper Warm River, is a rather isolated stream with small brookies. Moose Creek, accessible from FR 082 east of Macks Inn, closes August 15 to protect spawning kokanee salmon from Island Park Reservoir. When I was a kid, this wasn't the case, and dad and the gang would fish the creek for big rainbows during the fall.

Targhee Creek originates on the Continental Divide north of Henry's Lake and flows through the Targhee National Forest for six miles before entering private property on its way to the lake. This is hike-in-only water and the trail passes through spectacular country on its way over the divide.

A number of mountain lakes in the national forest offer good fishing for cutthroat and other species. Contact the IDFG for up-to-date status reports on Upper Goose Lake, Swan Lake and Horseshoe lake, the latter of which is stocked with grayling. Although small, these grayling are unique and beautiful fish.

In the Centennials north of Kilgore (east of Island Park) is one of the region's best small lakes. Aldous Lake has a reputation of offering cutthroat to near trophy sizes. Lug a float tube over the mile-long trail to fish the summer *Callibaetis* mayfly emergence.

A number of productive creeks drain the Idaho side of the Centennials. Cottonwood and East Camas Creek offer small, but willing trout; West Camas and Three-mile Creeks are larger and offer some decent fish. Last time I visited the area, Three-mile sported some great beaver ponds. All of these creeks flow through Forest Service lands in their upper reaches and ranchlands in their lower stretches. A knock on a door can get you permission to fish private lands.

South of Kilgore, Camas Creek enters a small desert canyon where brown trout have been planted in years past. Rumor suggests these fish attain impressive size, but in that neck of the woods I've typically been too busy chasing down sagehens to worry about the trout in the creek. If you're of a like mind, the Red Road runs north-south and bisects hundreds of square miles of prime sage grouse habitat. Towards its south end, the Red Road (named for the red cinder used in its construction) passes by the St. Anthony Sand Dunes. Sharptail grouse inhabit the more remote areas around the dunes. If that weren't enough, forest grouse

FRANK AMATO

thrive in the Centennials and Beaverheads. Look for ruffs along the creeks and seeps; hike the timbered ridgetops for blues.

West of the Camas Creek drainage, Medicine Lodge Creek flows southeasterly out of the Beaverhead Mountains. The best reaches lie primarily on private property, but to date access is available if you knock on a few doors. Cutthroat and rainbows inhabit the creek, with some fish reaching 18 inches. Hopper season is the perfect time to fish the upper meadows along Bannack Pass Road northwest of Dubois.

Many other small mountain streams provide good fishing for smaller trout and if you have a Montana license, drive over Bannack pass and fish Deadman Creek and the other streams on the north slope of the Beaverheads. A set of Targhee National Forest maps will guide you over all of this terrain—obtain the maps for the Dubois, Island Park, and Ashton ranger districts.

Sand Creek Ponds

Located 15 miles north of St. Anthony, the 15,000-acre Sand Creek Wildlife Management Area includes four ponds that offer good float-tube fishing for rainbows and brook trout that span 10 to 20 inches in length. To reach the ponds, exit Hwy. 20 at Fun Farm Road just northeast of St. Anthony, cross the river, then turn north on Sand Creek Road; or exit the highway at Youngs Corner, drive toward St. Anthony, cross the river and turn north on Sand Creek Road. Camping is available and current regulations forbid floating devices, including float tubes, until July 1, after the waterfowl have fledged. Motorized craft are not allowed. The ponds open Memorial Day weekend and close at the end of November.

GREG THOMAS

Big Lost River

The Big Lost River gathers its headwaters from the majestic Pioneer, White Knob and Boulder mountain ranges northeast of Sun Valley. After its forks converge at the foot of these ranges, the Big Lost River flows east across a sagebrush plain before emptying into Mackay Reservoir and eventually flowing south towards the deserts. In effect, the Big Lost offers two fisheries, the first being the freestone fishery above the reservoir as far upstream as the forks and their tributaries. The other fishery, and an increasingly popular one, is the tailwater fishery created by Mackay Dam.

Special regulations on the Big Lost upstream from Bartlett Point Road (above Mackay Reservoir) limit the take to two trout over 14 inches. This beautiful freestone river is a pleasure to wade and fish as are its tributaries above, including the North Fork, East Fork, Summit Creek and Wildhorse Creek. Star Hope Creek, the so-called West Fork of the Big Lost, originates in beautiful and popular Copper Basin—a narrow, scenic basin guarded by the high peaks of the Pioneer Mountains.

Despite its spectacular beauty and the majesty of the surrounding country, the Big Lost drainage is not what it used to be. Trout are few and far between. Still, those willing to do some walking can have entire mountain creeks all to themselves; nor is it unusual to find long reaches of the Big Lost below the forks devoid of other anglers.

The tailwater fishery below Mackay Reservoir is altogether different, for it has become quite popular owing to the large rainbows taken from its clear waters. You can access this tailwater fishery from two places, the first being immediately below the dam and the other being the sportsman's access area about two miles downstream. If you stay in the riverbed, you can fish between these two points. Camping sites are available at both sites as well and a fee campground is located at Mackay Reservoir.

Special regulations on the Big Lost drainage are aimed at restoring the river's wild-trout fishery.

Rainbow trout up to several pounds can be taken on dry-flies below the reservoir, especially when stoneflies hatch during July or when the cranefly and hopper action starts. Both hoppers and craneflies last well into September. For the latter, try skating a dry-fly through the tops of the riffles and underneath overhanging willows along the banks. *Baetis* and pale morning dun hatches can provide some dry-fly action as well. Otherwise, streamers and nymphs are productive. The river can run high well into June and early July after wet winters, so be sure to check with IDFG before venturing out early in the summer.

The trout-laden headwater tributaries of the Big Lost drain some of Idaho's most spectacular mountains.

Beautiful wild rainbows inhabit the scenic Big Lost River.

Hwy. 93 leads north from Arco and Trail Creek Road leads over Trail Creek Summit from Sun Valley. Trail Creek Road over the summit is gravel and is not maintained for passenger vehicles. The tailwater fishery below Mackay Reservoir is adjacent to Hwy. 93 a few miles north of Mackay. If you're headed to the upper river from Hwy. 93, drive past Mackay Reservoir about eight miles to Trail Creek Road, which turns off to the west. The road is paved up to Bartlett Point Road and gravel after that. Once you get above the ranches, you can fish anywhere and you'll find a network of rough dirt roads that lead through the sagebrush a short distance over to the river.

The tributaries are equally easy to access, although bear in mind that all the roads are gravel and some of them are rough. At the junction of Trail Creek Road and FR 135, near the East Fork confluence, you will find a big map and sign detailing the area and showing current regulations for fishing the various tributaries.

Little Lost River

This attractive little stream originates in part from the rivulets draining Idaho's highest mountains. Its upper waters harbor brook trout and rainbows, along with a unique population of land-locked Dolly Varden. Anglers intent on keeping brookies should be able to distinguish between these and the protected Dollies. Farther downstream, the Little Lost is primarily a rainbow fishery. Regulations limit the take to two trout per day above the confluence of Big Springs Creek, about 12 miles north of Howe. The Little Lost flows through a mix of both private and BLM lands, so be sure to ask permission if you're not sure about ownership of a particular reach. To reach the Little Lost, follow Hwy. 20 to its intersection with State Route 22/33 east of Arco. Turn northeast on 22/33 and proceed to the community of Howe and then turn north up the Little Lost. Consult the Challis National Forest Map for directions to the tributary streams.

Birch Creek

Birch Creek is a popular little high-plains stream flowing south through a broad valley. Much of this creek runs through private property, so be sure to ask permission. Naturally, the best fishing tends to be found on private property away from State Route 28, which follows the stream through

Birch Creek Valley. A 173-acre sportsman's access site (Kaufman) is located five miles north of Lone Pine. To reach Birch Creek, follow Hwy. 33 out of Rexburg (or follow I-15 north from Idaho Falls to Hwy. 33) and then turn north on Hwy. 28. From the west, follow Hwy. 20 to Hwy. 22/33 east of Arco. Follow 22/33 northeast past Howe. About eight miles east of Howe, Hwy. 22 will split off from 33 and swing to the northeast. Follow Hwy. 22 14 miles up to Hwy. 28 and turn north to reach Birch Creek.

The author fishes the head of a pool on the Big Lost River above Mackay Reservoir.

SOUTHEAST REGION

Existing in the shadow of the blue-ribbon fisheries to the north, the waters of the southeast region receive far less pressure from out-of-state anglers and thus offer some attractive options to the angler willing to explore new country. Some excellent stream fishing can be found on the Blackfoot River and on countless small streams that drain the Salt River system. Many other creeks flow through the Bear River Range, Portneuf Range, Bannock Range and the Deep Creek Mountains. This is the country where I learned to fly fish and while I'm not about to rattle off the names of my favorite trout-filled, beaver-dammed creeks, I will say that they are not hard to find. Get some good maps and start exploring.

You will find little mountain streams, many with beaver dams and others winding through aspen-lined ravines, where native cutthroat predominate, but where an occasional brookie, brown, or rainbow trout shows up as well. Southeast Idaho offers some incredible country with an abundance of wildlife.

Once this land was home to the Shoshone and Bannock tribes. Today the Fort Hall Reservation is home to these peoples, but their mark is left on the land in the form of ancient petroglyphs and scattered arrow and dart points. Through the Fort Hall Reservation flows some of the region's best spring creeks—the Fort Hall Bottoms.

Some historical confusion exists as to the so-called Bannocks. Sven Liljeblad, a leading expert on the Shoshone, relates that the Bannock were simply Northern Paiutes from Oregon who joined the Shoshone on buffalo hunting expeditions to the plains. These people integrated with the Shoshone and the two groups learned each other's language.

Liljeblad says, "Speakers of Paiute called themselves *pannakwaty.* The origin of this term is complex and uncertain, but writing gentlemen among the white fur traders rendered it in a variety of forms—"Pannacks," Banniques," or "Bonacks"—and the name ultimately became "Bannock."

"These white men," Liljeblad continues, "understood the word to be the native designation of an independent tribe. This misunderstanding remained both in the literature and in the popular local tradition, and today the word is used ambiguously." (The Idaho Heritage, ISU Press, 1974).

The Fort Hall Reservation, where many of the Shoshone Peoples were ultimately compelled to reside, more or less surrounds Pocatello. Pocatello is the largest city in the southeast region and it offers all needed services. Other regional attractions include Lava Hot Springs, where natural hot springs have been captured in pools so tourists and locals alike can soak up the mineral warmth on cool winter days and nights.

FRANK AMATO

Gray's Lake, to the northeast of Pocatello, was home to a whooping crane recovery effort during the 1970s and 80s. Their numbers down to some 50 or so wild birds, whooping cranes were on the verge of extinction. In an attempt to build a new flock, biologists placed whooping crane eggs in the nests of resident sandhill cranes at Gray's Lake hoping that the sandhills would successfully lead the whoopers to the wintering grounds, where they could flock with others of their kind. Unfortunately, the whooping cranes that were raised by foster-parent sandhill cranes never figured out that they were whooping cranes. Thus they never attempted to pair up and breed with other whoopers.

Gray's Lake National Wildlife Refuge, which spans 18,300 acres, is also home to the largest number of and highest density of nesting sandhill cranes in the Rocky Mountain region. In addition to the cranes, the refuge is home to nesting trumpeter and tundra swans, along with many varieties of ducks, geese and other birds. The Bear Lake Refuge, similarly, is an important nesting area for cranes, swans, geese, ducks and other fowl.

Traditionally, the main draw for fly anglers in the Southeast Region has been the 30-odd irrigation storage reservoirs whose fisheries are managed carefully by IDFG. Several of these—Daniels, 24-Mile and Treasureton reservoirs—are managed for trophy trout and as such are fly/artificial-only waters. Others, such as Hawkins, Chesterfield and Little Valley can, at times, offer excellent fishing for large trout despite being open to all forms of sport tackle. Many of the reservoirs are managed as warm-water fisheries and, owing to water quality problems, could not support healthy trout populations.

In fact, water quality is one of the major challenges facing fisheries managers in southeast Idaho, where rivers like the Portneuf and Bear have for generations been exploited for their agricultural value. Nonetheless, anglers visiting southeast Idaho will find plenty to choose from, especially if they bring with them a willingness to get off the beaten path.

Blackfoot River

The upper Blackfoot River has become quite a story in southeast Idaho. Once the domain of cutthroat spawning runs numbering in the hundreds of thousands of individuals, the river's trout population had essentially collapsed by the mid-1980s.

The river was dammed in 1909, creating an effluvial cutthroat fishery. The fish matured in 19,000-acre Blackfoot Reservoir, then ascended the river to spawn in tributaries as far as 60 miles upstream. These tremendous spawning runs, which included lots of cutthroat over eight pounds, were living on borrowed time.

By the 1950s, the trout were subjected to heavy harvest by reservoir anglers. Meanwhile, the water in the Blackfoot drainage was being increasingly diverted to agriculture and in many places cattle grazed the riparian vegetation into non-existence. Already suffering, with its tremendous cutthroat run in decline, the river was struck a near-fatal blow when a severe drought cycle hit during the late 1970s. The fishery was devastated.

My familiarity with the upper Blackfoot—or the region at least—began during those drought years of the early 1980s when I began hunting grouse in the surrounding Caribou National Forest, especially the Webster Range whose tiny streams feed the river's headwaters. Like many other anglers over the years, I looked longingly at the spectacular meadows owned by the Stocking Ranch. Here the Blackfoot meanders in wide S-curves through a broad valley that, during the grouse season, glows amber in the early morning sun.

In 1995, the Idaho Department of Fish & Game finalized its purchase of this magnificent piece of property. IDFG created a management area here that today offers public access to some seven miles of the Upper Valley, through which the Blackfoot River meanders. While IDFG was working out the Stocking Ranch purchase during the early 1990s, the severe drought came to an end and cutthroat runs returned to the river, not in the hundreds of thousands, but at least in the thousands.

The hope now is that by working out grazing deals with area ranchers, by re-vitalizing the river's waterway and riparian zone, and by carefully managing the sport fishery on both the reservoir and the upstream drainage, the Blackfoot River will again become a blue-ribbon cutthroat

trout stream. Already the fishing is much improved on the river, not only because cutthroat populations are recovering but also because public access is much improved with the IDFG's purchase of Stocking Ranch.

The best fishing occurs on the Stocking Ranch property and good fishing is available just below the valley in the Upper Narrows, a reach of about three miles where the river's gradient steepens through a small canyon. At the bottom of the canyon, the Blackfoot enters another valley (Lower Valley), where access is very limited by extensive private land. If you add up all the river miles from Slug Creek Bridge below The Narrows up to the access at the top end of Stocking Ranch, including the wide meanders in the Upper Valley, you are left with a section of public access reminiscent of the Box Canyon through Harriman reach on the Henry's Fork. And with continued good water supply and foresighted management, perhaps the fishery here will soon gain a similar reputation.

To protect the spawning fish, which ascend the river during late May and June, the river does not open until July 1. This means that anglers miss out on most of the giant stonefly hatch, although some years see the hatch last into early July. Golden stoneflies occur in The Narrows and in a few other reaches. Caddis are abundant and provide exceptional evening hatches. October caddis (giant orange sedge) hatch during September. Mayfly hatches are also prevalent, especially blue-winged olives and pale morning duns. Cool, overcast days offer the best mayfly hatches. During most of the season, terrestrial patterns can prove especially effective; these include hopper, ant and beetle patterns.

The entire section from the headwaters down to the top of Lower Valley offers expansive classic dry-fly water, ranging from the glassy flats on the Stocking Ranch to the pocket water glides of The Narrows. Despite its potential for the dry-fly enthusiast, some anglers enjoy fishing streamers and wet-flies for the big cutthroat. Favorites include leech patterns, Woolly Buggers, Zonkers, big Renegades and many others.

During July, the river still has lots of cutthroat that have not yet returned to the reservoir below. Thus, even though an average Blackfoot River trout might span 10 to 12 inches, you still have a better than average chance of finding fish in the 16- to 24-inch range. A number of these fish stick around in the upper river all summer and into fall and as the trout population increases, late summer and autumn should increasingly offer excellent prospects for large cutthroat.

In addition to the public access area from Stocking Ranch down through The Narrows, anglers can usually gain permission to cross private lands farther downstream. Typically this won't be necessary, as you can find plenty of open water above. Also, noted Idaho Falls author Bruce Staples says that a big run of spawning carp tend to discolor the water in the downstream reaches. Besides, gaining permission to cross private lands in the Lower Valley and actually getting to the water can be two different things, depending on where you choose to walk.

The Stocking Ranch property lies some 30 miles northeast of Soda Springs. From Pocatello and points south, Take I-15 and Hwy. 30 out to Soda Springs (about 55 miles), then turn north on Hwy. 34 at the east edge of town. Follow Hwy. 34 due north about 12 miles until you reach its intersection with Blackfoot River Road. Turn right and head upriver, through Lower Valley and through The Narrows and on up to Stocking Ranch. (Blackfoot River Road will become FR 095/Lanes Creek Road when you reach the Caribou National Forest boundary). Parking areas for the Stocking Ranch are located at both ends, the lower lot being a short distance beyond the junction with FR 121; the upper lot, less than two miles further on FR 102.

From the Idaho Falls area, you can get to the Stocking Ranch area by any of several rural secondary roads, including Long Valley Road over to Gray's Lake. Consult a county map. Although longer than the rural road routes, you can head up the South Fork of the Snake, cross over into Wyoming and turn south on Hwy. 89. From Alpine (junction of Hwy. 26/89) drive south about 14 miles to Route 239, which crosses the Salt River and access the town of Freedom. Turn north at Freedom, drive one mile and turn west on Hwy. 34. (There is, of course, some excellent fishing to be had on the Salt River, so if you're not careful you may never get to the Blackfoot.) Follow Hwy. 34 west approximately 15 miles to FR 095 and turn left. From the Hwy. 34/FR 095 junction you are only about 10 miles from Stocking Ranch.

Lots of rough camping is available in the Caribou National Forest and five small campgrounds are located in the area, the closest being Mill Canyon Campground located along The Narrows just downstream from the Stocking Ranch. Gravel Creek Campground is several miles to the north, in the Gray's Range. Pine Bar and Tincup Campgrounds lie along Hwy. 34 between FR 095 and Freedom, Wyoming, and Diamond Creek Camp is located some 12 miles to the southeast on Diamond Creek Road (FR 102).

Portneuf River

The Portneuf River above Lava Hot Springs doesn't have much to offer these days, although at one time it was a good trout stream. You can still catch a few decent trout during good water years. Public access is available at three IDFG sites north of Lava Hot Springs (Lower Portneuf, Upper Portneuf and Mike's Place). Tributaries, including Toponce Creek and Pebble Creek offer fine small-stream fishing for trout that will rarely exceed a foot in length. Some beaver-pond fishing is available on both drainages. These tributaries can be reached via Old Hwy. 30 and Kelly-Toponce Road. Turn north on Old Hwy. 30 just east of Lava Hot Springs.

The Portneuf River below Lava Hot Springs (along Hwy. 30) still offers fairly decent fishing for rainbows and brown trout, especially if the water clears up during fall. Some 20 years ago I enjoyed good fishing on the Portneuf in Marsh Valley between Robber's Roost and Rapid Creek; likewise, the tributaries off the Scout Mountain area to the west used to be good, too. I haven't explored these places in two decades, but a little legwork might go a long way.

Fort Hall Bottoms

The Fort Hall Bottoms area lies on the Fort Hall Reservation and offers some of the region's top spring-creek fishing on streams that empty into American Falls Reservoir. You will need a tribal fishing permit to fish these waters. For specific directions and details, check with the tribal fish & game office and with All Seasons Angler in Pocatello.

Daniels Reservoir

Probably the best known of southeast Idaho's "float-tube" waters, Daniels Reservoir is managed as a trophy trout water where rainbows, hybrids, and cutthroat grow very fast. Trout over 20 inches are common during good years, with fish of six to eight pounds taken regularly when ample water is available and when chub populations are under control.

This 375-acre reservoir is rich in aquatic life, with dense populations of protein-rich scuds that allow trout to gain pounds and inches quickly. Damsels, water beetles, snails, leeches and all the other usual suspects abound in Daniels' fertile, weedy soup. Look for the damsel hatch during early July, followed soon thereafter by *Callibaetis* hatches. Excellent Chironomid emergences occur early and late in the year as well as just about every morning and evening throughout the season.

Daniels Reservoir is perfect for float tubing and indeed tubers comprise a majority of the anglers on any given day. During the first light of early morning, look for trout cruising the shoreline in just inches of water as they root around for scuds and beetles. These shoreline feeders can be very challenging, requiring a careful approach and a perfect cast. I've seen countless bonefish that are far less spooky.

Don't rule out night fishing at Daniels or at the other southeast Idaho reservoirs. When I lived in southeast Idaho during the 1970s, we habitually stayed out until well after dark, trolling or stripping big black leech patterns from our float tubes. Some of the biggest fish and most ferocious strikes came at night.

To reach Daniels, follow I-15 south out of Pocatello (or north from Utah) to Malad City and then turn northwest on West Daniels Road, which will take you directly to the reservoir. If you don't mind gravel roads, a shorter route to Daniels leads from Hawkins Reservoir (which see) over to Dairy Creek Road and down to Daniels. Follow I-15 to Exit 36 and then head west on Hawkins Road about nine miles to Hawkins Reservoir. Turn left just below the dam onto Sheep Creek Road (gravel), which joins Dairy Creek Road southeast of the reservoir and then continues on down to Daniels Reservoir. A campground is located at the reservoir.

Daniels Reservoir.

Tim Blount battles a big rainbow on Chesterfield Reservoir.

Hawkins Reservoir

Hawkins Reservoir is a popular 54-acre trout reservoir located southwest of Garden Creek Gap in the Bannock Range south of Pocatello. The perfect size for float tubing, Hawkins can produce rainbows to 20 inches or more during years of good water supply. To reach Hawkins, follow Interstate 15 south out of Pocatello, past the Lava Hot Springs turnoff, and turn west off the freeway at Exit 36. Drive west about nine miles to the reservoir. Campsites, outhouses, and a ramp are located at the reservoir.

Chesterfield Reservoir

At full pool, which it rarely accomplishes, Chesterfield Reservoir covers 1,600 acres in the foothills draining the upper Portneuf River and the Portneuf Range. During good water years, Chesterfield's rainbow trout can grow very quickly. Fish weighing two to five pounds are typical and rainbows up to eight pounds are available.

Chesterfield Reservoir is not covered by any special regulations so many of its fish end their days dangling from a stringer. Most fly anglers who visit Chesterfield regularly wouldn't mind seeing a slot limit or other restrictions enacted so the fishing would hold up better through the season, especially during low-water years. Likely this won't happen any time soon. Fortunately, Chesterfield is just far enough off the beaten path that when water supply is good and the chubs haven't infested the lake, fishing holds up well into fall and fly anglers have a good shot at some truly remarkable trout. Ice-off usually occurs during April and the fishing can last through October and into November.

The upper end of Chesterfield Reservoir lies within the Fort Hall Indian Reservation so a tribal permit is required. Don't bother with that—most of the reservoir lies south of the reservation and plenty of trout can be taken along the shoreline margins adjacent to the access road and dam. Despite its size, Chesterfield is a good float-tube reservoir. Spring and fall midge hatches can be profuse. Damsels, dragons, water beetles, backswimmers, boatmen and *Callibaetis* mayflies are abundant. During much of the year, especially during spring and fall, a deep-fished leech pattern

will take lots of trout. Also try scud imitations (olive green and olive-tan in sizes 10-16). These crustaceans are abundant in the lake and probably form the single most important year-round food item in the trout's diet.

To reach Chesterfield Reservoir, follow I-15 south out of Pocatello, exiting the freeway at the McCammon/Lava Hot Springs turnoff (Hwy. 30). Just east of Lava Hot Springs, turn north on Old Highway 30 and follow the highway some 10 miles to a left turn called Kelly-Toponce Road. Follow this road another 10 miles to the signed turnoff for Chesterfield Reservoir (Nipper Road). If you are coming from the south on Hwy. 30, turn right onto Old Hwy. 30 at the Hwy. 30/34 intersection north of Grace. Follow the old highway to Bancroft and turn right in town, heading toward the old Chesterfield Townsite. Follow this road through the Chesterfield Townsite (and past the turnoff to 24-Mile Reservoir) until you reach Nipper Road. A good ramp is located on the southwest corner above the dam (along the access road) and easy float-tube launches abound.

During good water years, when chub populations are down, Chesterfield and other southeast Idaho reservoirs will be at their best, producing rainbows like this.

24-mile Reservoir is one of several productive irrigation-storage reservoirs in southeast Idaho.

24-mile Reservoir

This 50-acre, special-regulations reservoir sits in an aspen-lined bowl in the Chesterfield Range a few miles east of Chesterfield Reservoir. Follow the directions above for Chesterfield Reservoir, but continue past the turnoff on Nipper Road and drive about five miles to the old Chesterfield Townsite. Turn northeast at a signed gravel road and wind your way four miles up to the reservoir.

Because of its elevation, 24-mile Reservoir has a shorter algae-bloom season than Chesterfield, so fishing holds up later into summer and begins earlier in the fall. This is another very fertile reservoir with dense populations of scuds, beetles, snails, leeches, damsels and mayflies. 24-mile is artificials-only and is managed as a trophy trout lake. Rainbows to 20 inches are common during good years and the lake grows some big cutthroat, hybrids and a few brook trout.

Treasureton Reservoir

Treasureton Reservoir is one of southeast Idaho's top artificials-only reservoirs, producing trout to 24 inches during good years. As with the other southeast Idaho reservoirs, a good year is defined by good water supply and a controlled or eliminated chub population.

Southeast Idaho's irrigation storage reservoirs are rich in aquatic trout foods, none more significant than the scuds that allow trout to grow at a rate of an inch or more per month.

Planted rainbows from the Hayspur Hatchery and rainbow-cutthroat hybrids from Henry's Lake are stocked in Treasureton and both species grow quickly on the 150-acre reservoir's abundant food supply. Trout planted at eight to nine inches will reach 15 to 16 inches during their first year. Historically, Bonneville cutthroat inhabited this drainage, but these are mostly a memory now.

Scuds are a significant part of the trout's diet in Treasureton and all the other forage organisms are abundant as well, including damsels, water beetles, mayflies, leeches, and Chironomids. A strong damsel emergence begins during June and lasts most of the summer (peaking during late June and early July). Fish damsel nymph imitations during mid-morning around near-shore weed beds and reed stands. Still days can offer some of the region's best dry damsel fishing as well. The *Callibaetis* mayflies (speckled wing duns) hatch during the summer, as well, often providing good dry-fly action. Try a size 14 *Callibaetis* Sparkle Dun or Gulper Special. Chironomids hatch all season long.

A heavy algae bloom usually hits the reservoir midsummer, reducing visibility to just a few feet. Fishing can still be quite good, especially for those who remember that night fishing is legal. Also, draw-down for irrigation can be substantial, especially during lean water years. The reservoir typically freezes in December and thaws during March or early April.

Access from the north is from Hwy. 91, which turns off Interstate 15 some 12 miles south of the McCammom/Lava Hot Springs Exit. Follow Hwy. 91 south to Oxford Road, which leads east to Route 34. The reservoir is a mile to the south. Or follow Hwy. 91 past Oxford Road some 3.5 miles down to Mail Route Road, which leads northeast to the reservoir.

Bear River

The Bear River is a stream that has long been used for the needs of agriculture with little regard to anything else. As a result, only a few sections of this lengthy river system offer viable trout fisheries today, the best being the Black Canyon section off Hwy. 34 southeast of Lava Hot Springs.

The Black Canyon reach is de-watered to a hydro-power canal, but the lower two miles are supplemented by 50 to 80 cfs (cubic feet per second) of cold spring water that provides ample and fertile habitat for rainbow trout and the few cutthroats. This is good dry-fly water with pools formed by lava pockets and lots of good boulder-strewn holding water. Caddis, stoneflies and terrestrials abound. During summer, aquatic vegetation is rather lush, this fishery typically offers year-round opportunity.

The fishable stretch lies above the Grace Power Plant, southwest of the tiny community of Grace. Follow Hwy. 30 to Hwy. 34 and turn south until you reach Grace. Turn west on Center Street or drive past the high school and LDS church to the south end of town and turn west on One-mile Road. Follow either of these roads a short distance to River Road and turn left (south). Drive about 2.5 miles until you see the sign announcing Grace Power Plant and Training Center (Varley Road). Turn west and follow Varley Road about a mile down to the power plant. As you reach the bottom of the hill approaching the power plant residences, veer left at the first Y-intersection then drive about a hundred yards and turn right at the next street. Follow this route past the training center, over a cattle guard and about 1/4 mile to a gravel parking area on the left. A footbridge crosses the river and a trail follows the west bank. Watch for rattlers.

Two other good stretches of the Bear River are the tailwaters below both Alexander and Oneida dams. These sections are planted with rainbows and brown trout and also offer remnant populations of Bonneville cutthroat. The rainbows are planted at catchable size; the browns at four to five inches. Ten- to 12-inch trout are typical, but carry-overs reach 20 inches. Both offer lots of good dry-fly water characterized by rubble/boulder habitat with lots of pockets and pools.

Access is good for both reaches with the section below Alexander Dam being a walk-in deal that assures light fishing pressure. Alexander Dam is located near the little wide spot of Alexander a few miles west of Soda Springs and about two miles east of the Hwy. 30/34 junction.

The Black Canyon of the Bear River offers good year-round trout fishing in southeast Idaho.

Oneida Dam lies approximately 30 miles to the south of Alexander and east of Hwy. 34. You can get there just as easily by following I-15 to Hwy. 91 and then heading south until you reach the town of Preston. Then continue east and north for a few miles until you reach the junction of Hwy. 34 and Route 36. Turn east on 36 and proceed about three miles up to Oneida Narrows/Bear River Road, which parallels the river up to the dam. Owing to the easy road access, this section receives fairly heavy angling pressure.

Summer irrigation results in fluctuating flows in both the Alexander and Oneida Dam tailwater fisheries, so fishing that time of year is unpredictable. Between October and March or April, however, water levels remain stable and fishing can be quite good. If you can hit either section during good water years, the hopper fishing can be explosive during July, August, and September. Both reservoirs, incidentally, are warm-water fisheries, with Oneida having perch and walleye and Alexander offering a few wild cutthroat along with perch and catfish.

Preston/Malad City Area Warmwater Reservoirs

Several reservoirs near Preston and Malad can offer good fishing for a variety of species, especially during good water years. Weston Reservoir (112 acres) and Winder Reservoir (94 acres) offer planted rainbow trout

along with largemouth bass and perch. Winder also has bluegill. Both are notable for their no-boats restriction that makes float tubes the only permissible watercraft. Although carry-over trout can attain impressive size at times, these two waters are better for bass fishing. Winder is north of Preston, off Winder Reservoir Road and Weston lies southeast of Malad City along Deep Creek Road (southeast of the Deep Creek Reservoir).

North of Winder Reservoir is 117-acre Condie Reservoir, which features rainbow trout, bass, bluegill and perch. Additionally, IDFG planted 100 foot-long tiger muskies in the fall of 1995. Might be a good one to keep an eye on for that reason. The ever-popular Twin Lakes Reservoir (446 acres) is located on the west side of Hwy. 91, due west of Winder Reservoir. Twin Lakes typically offers good fishing for bass and bluegill and also produces some big rainbows. Until it was poisoned in 1993 to eradicate carp, Twin Lakes was among the state's top warm-water fisheries. Having been re-planted, this reservoir should again return to its former productivity.

Foster, Glendale and Johnson are similar, offering rainbows, largemouth bass, perch and bluegill. These three reservoirs lie just to the northeast of Preston. Foster covers 145 surface acres at full pool; Glendale, 230 acres; and Johnson, 50 acres.

Bear Lake

Beautiful Bear Lake straddles the Idaho-Utah border south of Montpelier and at 70,000 surface acres is one of the largest natural lakes in the Rockies. Bonneville (Bear Lake) cutthroat are native inhabitants whose numbers are supplemented by hatchery stocks. These cutthroat are native to only two places in Idaho, one being Bear Lake, the other being the Thomas Fork drainage of the Bear River. Lake trout are stocked in Bear Lake, as well, and these reproduce in very limited numbers.

Although not really a fly-fishing destination, Bear Lake can nonetheless provide good fishing for 12- to 20-plus-inch cutthroat. The lake is shaped like an oblong oval, oriented north to south, and has no coves or bays to speak of. Thus the best fly angling occurs in the near-shore shallows early and late in the year. You won't find much competition from fellow fly anglers.

Except for the mouth of St. Charles Creek on the northwest shore, the entire lake is open year-round, though a typical winter brings a three-month ice cover between January and March. An area extending 300 yards beyond the mouth of St. Charles Creek is closed from April 15 to July 1 to protect spawning cutthroat.

Hwy. 89 parallels the lake's west shoreline and Eastside Lake Road follows the east shore, so access is good. The Bear Lake National Wildlife Refuge occupies the lake's northern outlet area, including Mud Lake, which is separated from Bear Lake by a narrow isthmus. To reach Eastside Lake Road from Hwy. 89, turn east at the village of St. Charles on Turnpike Road and follow the north shore of the lake for about six miles. Bear Lake State Park features two public ramps, one at East Beach Unit on the east shore, about two miles north of the Utah border; the other at North Beach Unit on the north shore. A fee ramp is located at Fish Haven on the west shore south of St. Charles.

Cub River

The little Cub River drains a portion of the west slope of the Bear River Range, flowing southwest into Utah. Private land surrounds the river for most of its length and it is heavily de-watered in its lower reaches anyway. Thus, the best fishing is found above Moser Campground in the Cache National Forest. Although rainbow trout from Hayspur Hatchery are planted at Willow Flat Campground, the majority of the river is managed for wild Bonneville cutthroat that average nine to 10 inches and reach 16 inches.

Access to the Cub River is from Highway 91 south of Preston. About two miles south of Whitney, watch for Cub River Road leading east from the highway. Follow this road about eight miles up to the national forest boundary and fish from here on up the river. Interstate 15 out of Pocatello will take you to Hwy. 91. Nearby Mink Creek is worth fishing

Southeast Idaho's stillwater fisheries produce rainbows to trophy sizes.

as long as you are in the area and you can follow a trail from Willow Flat Campground up the Cub River's headwaters and over the divide to beautiful Bloomington Lake (see below). High Line Trail follows the top of the divide and you can hike to the top of 9,311-foot Bloomington Peak and 9,216-foot Cub Peak, both of which reward climbers with commanding views of Bear Lake and the surrounding country.

Bloomington Lake

A beautiful little mountain lake, Bloomington is nestled against rocky crags in the Wasatch Range northwest of Bear Lake. This 10-acre gem reminds one of alpine lakes found in the Sawtooths of central Idaho or other such places. Its planted cutthroat rarely grow large, but the setting makes up for that fact. Easiest access to Bloomington Lake is from the town of Bloomington on Hwy. 89 a few miles north of Bear Lake. Forest Service Road 409 turns west at the south end of town and follows Bloomington Creek some six miles up to the national forest boundary. Here the road degrades to a reasonably good dirt number and leads another six miles up to the short trail into the lake. The creek can be fun to fish for small cutthroat. Nearby Bloomington, Paris, and Cub Peaks offer exceptional views of the Bear Lake country. Climb them early in the morning.

St. Charles Creek

An important Bear Lake spawning tributary, St. Charles Creek offers good catch-and-release fishing for cutthroat (and some brook trout, depending on where you are fishing). Because most spawning occurs in the stream's lower reaches, the section from Bear Lake up to the national forest boundary is closed from the end of November to the first of July. Several campgrounds are located along the creek and Minnetonka Cave (follow the signs) is well worth seeing for its curious limestone formations. Paris Ice Cave, west of the little town of Paris, is another of the area's interesting natural attractions.

Little Valley Reservoir

During good water years, this 32-acre reservoir can produce rainbows and cutthroat to 18-plus inches. Little Valley is perfect float-tube water, although fishing from shore can be just as productive. Scuds, damsels, leeches, Chironomids, water beetles and the other usual suspects are all plentiful. Follow Hwy. 89 south to the town of Paris. Drive south past the LDS church and turn west on Creamery Road or on Canyon Road. The reservoir is about five miles from town. (To reach Highway 89 and Paris, follow Hwy. 30 to Montpelier and turn west on 89.)

MAGIC VALLEY REGION

The Magic Valley Region is aptly named, for this part of Idaho offers many a magical experience for fly anglers in pursuit of quality angling amidst beautiful scenery. The regions crown jewel is Silver Creek, the famed spring creek whose dense mayfly hatches and large rainbows combine to offer some of the world's most cherished dry-fly fishing. Nearby is the Big Wood River, which has, in essence, become an urban fishery as it flows north to south through Sun Valley and the quaint little hamlets of Ketchum, Hailey and Bellevue. Here the celebrities come to play, mostly during the winter when the famous ski runs are deep in powder. Yet the Big Wood remains an exceptional freestone fishery.

Other fisheries of the area are productive as well: Magic Reservoir, which during times of good water supply can produce good still-water fishing for brown trout; Beartracks Preserve on the Little Wood River, where large brown trout await anglers armed with streamers and mouse patterns.

To the south, along the Snake River, lies the beautiful Hagerman Valley where commercial trout farms abound owing to a tremendous underground aquifer. Springs bubble to the surface throughout the valley, the most impressive of which burst from the bluffs above the Snake River at Thousand Springs. Riley Creek and Hagerman Creek have traditionally lured anglers to this area, although problems with water quality and reductions in flow have substantially altered the fishery. This so-called "banana belt" remains largely unfrozen during the winter because of the abundant springs and thus attracts Idaho's largest concentration of migrating and wintering waterfowl.

Geographically, the Magic Valley Region encompasses an expansive and diverse area. The Snake River flows through the heart of the region, even providing some fly angling opportunity at a few locations.

South of the Snake, however, you find the Bruneau River drainage, including the Bruneau itself, the East Fork of the Bruneau, and the Jarbridge River, all flowing south to north out of Nevada and through awesome desert canyons. The rivers converge in Owyhee County before eventually reaching the Snake River at C.J. Strike Reservoir. This arid land of the southwestern corner of the state is dominated by the rugged Owyhee Mountains, once home to fervent silver- and gold-mining activity. Today, this country offers the ultimate in solitude for those willing to explore the remote reaches of its desert streams.

GREG THOMAS

Silver Creek

Silver Creek is a name synonymous with Western spring creeks, it is the archetypal water of its kind. Flowing in gentle curves through a broad valley, Silver Creek gathers its waters from springs throughout its upper drainage. These springs define Silver Creek as a classic spring creek, where water levels and temperatures are stable, immense rooted vegetation harbors abundant insect life, and where tremendous hatches provide classic and challenging smooth-water, dry-fly fishing.

Despite its fame and productivity today, Silver Creek would never have regained its status as one of the great spring creek trout fisheries if not for the efforts of The Nature Conservancy. After liberal trout harvest and changing land use practices sent the once-renowned fishery into decline between the 1950s and early 1970s, The Nature Conservancy of Idaho (in 1975) purchased 480 acres of land, including two miles of the creek itself. This became The Nature Conservancy's Silver Creek Preserve. Since that time, the Conservancy has expanded its protection efforts to 32 miles of stream and more than 9,200 acres along Silver Creek and its tributaries. The original preserve now spans 825 acres and the Conservancy has worked hard at striking agreements with local landowners who have donated more than 8,000 acres of conservation easements.

The original Silver Creek Preserve is the destination for most fly anglers. Here the stream meanders in wide curves across lush meadows.

On the heavily fished flat waters of Silver Creek, stealth and delicacy pay dividends.

Accurate downstream presentations are the rule when fishing to Silver Creek's sophisticated trout.

The preserve is open to catch-and-release, fly-angling-only, and its abundance of rainbow trout that feed on dense hatches assure a steady and increasing stream of visitors each year.

When you visit this water for the first time, be prepared with both tactics and patterns that are appropriate for the smooth waters of a heavily fished spring creek. A careful, quiet approach is needed and only after you have picked a particular trout to which you will cast. Flock-shooting rarely works. Downstream presentations produce best, and flies should be tied to match specific hatches. Typically, leaders and tippets must be long and light.

Also, be prepared to match the hatches that will occur at the time you intend to visit. Hatches on Silver Creek, like those on other spring creeks, are fairly predictable in their timing and duration from year to year.

Fishing Silver Creek is more like hunting than angling. You pick a spot, wait for the trout to begin rising, and then pick out one fish at a time on which to try your skills. Excessive wading is considered bad form as it interferes with other anglers who are stalking other fish. Likewise, crowding another angler should be avoided, the distance you allow will largely be dictated by the number of anglers on the water that day. When in doubt, ask whether you can fish to a particular fish or position yourself in a particular place. A little common sense and a dose of courtesy go a long way on crowded waters like Silver Creek.

That is not to say that this stream is always crowded. July and August generally bring the largest crowds, but even then I've enjoyed many occasions when the creek was devoid of anglers. During a July trip not too long ago, Forrest Maxwell and I fished over a tremendous pale morning dun hatch that began at dusk—long after almost everyone else had departed. Sure the popular morning fishing had been good, but the PMD hatch that night was far better and we had it to ourselves. Similarly, you can avoid the summer crowds by fishing Silver Creek during fall.

Of course there is more to Silver Creek than just the preserve. Many anglers launch float tubes at Kilpatrick Bridge or at the launch site north of Lower Slough (upstream from the bridge). The lower end of the preserve down to Kilpatrick Bridge and the Purdy Ranch waters offers ideal float-tube conditions as the creek becomes a big, wide, slow-moving pond. If you float tube the section below the bridge, you must stay in the water and off the banks, which are private property.

Additional public access is found downstream (Silver Creek West Access and Point of Rocks Access) north of Hwy. 20. While these stretches are open to other forms of angling, harvest is still restricted and fly angling for big rainbows and brown trout can be excellent.

Silver Creek Preserve is accessed via Hwy. 20 a few miles east of the Hwy. 20/Hwy. 75 intersection. You can get to the preserve by turning south on Stalker Creek Road, five miles east of the Hwy. 20/75 intersection, or by continuing another two miles east until Hwy. 20 bends to the southeast and then turning south at the signed road leading to Silver

Creek Preserve and Kilpatrick Bridge (the turnoff is just east of the signed turnoff to Hayspur Fish Hatchery). Both entrances to the preserve lead by gravel back to the visitor's center building where anglers must sign-in before entering the property. Numerous trails lead through the preserve and anglers are asked to stay on these trails to avoid damaging the riparian vegetation. In several places, the banks have been so heavily trampled that restoration projects are underway—signs will tell you which areas are closed to foot traffic.

You will find ample parking at the visitor's center and also along the shoulder of the road leading up to the building from the east. If you park along the road, don't forget to first sign-in at the visitor's center, where you will find a logbook against the outside wall, along with a map and usually a volunteer or two who can answer any questions about the property.

The other Silver Creek access points are located north of Hwy. 20. To reach the west access, follow Hwy. 20 east until you cross the creek and then watch for a sportsman's access sign just before milepost 187. The east access (Point of Rocks) can be reached via this same road—just continue past the sportsman's access signs that lead to the west access and follow the road north and then east until you see the signs for the east access. Rough camping is available at both places. Rough camping is also available at Hayspur Hatchery. Just turn north off the highway at the road leading up to the hatchery and you'll see a grassy camping area a short distance up the road on your left.

All other services, including guides and fly shops, are available in Ketchum and Hailey. Just follow Hwy. 75 north. Picabo store has gas and supplies as well and is located a few miles east of Silver Creek Preserve on Hwy. 20.

Incidentally, if you enjoy Silver Creek and wish to lend a financial hand to its continued preservation and restoration, you might consider joining The Nature Conservancy of Idaho. The address is P.O. Box 165, Sun Valley, ID 83353.

Silver Creek Hatch Chart

MAYFLIES	TIMES	NOTES
Pale Morning Dun (*Ephemerella*)	June-August	Evening hatches during summer; dusk and after during hot weather; spinner falls a.m.; size 16-18
Brown Drake (*Ephemera simulans*)	early June	Typically hatches at dusk and thereafter; best on sections north of Hwy. 20; size 8-10
Baetis (blue-winged olives)	All season	Best hatches May-July and during fall; summer hatches usually mornings; autumn hatches late morning through late afternoon; intensity and duration of hatch generally depends on weather, with cloudy days best (size 18-22)
Tiny Western Olive (*Baetis*)	Late September	Size 22-24
Callibaetis (Speckled-wing dun)	June-September	Usually best on slow reaches and sloughs; consistent by July; mid-morning to mid-afternoon; size 14-18.
Tricos	July-August	Morning hatches/spinner falls; size 20-22
Mahogany Dun (*Paraleptophlebia*)	September	Midday; size 16.
Caddis (various)	June-Sept.	Numerous genera and species: Carry down-wing patterns and pupa patterns, size 14-20 in olive, tan and dark gray.
Terrestrials	June-September	Small ant and beetle patterns can be very effective; also hoppers and adult damsels.

The "Conservancy Water" on Silver Creek.

Big Wood River

At one time the Big Wood River trickled humbly down from the Boulder Mountains, through Sun Valley and Ketchum, on through Hailey and Bellevue, and into Magic Reservoir, all the while playing a distant second to its super-famous neighbor, Silver Creek. Those days are long gone. The Big Wood is a popular place these days, largely due to the sprawling growth of Sun Valley and surrounding communities.

A fine rainbow trout fishery in its own right, the Big Wood offers stark contrast to Silver Creek. Where Silver Creek is the archetypal spring creek with its naturally regulated flows, constant temperatures and low gradient, the Big Wood is classic Rocky Mountain freestone—emanating from the rugged crags; voluminous and raging during the spring runoff, a comparative trickle by late summer.

Hard-won progressive management strategies are paying dividends on the Big Wood, where rainbows average 12 to 16 inches with a few fishes reaching 20 or more. This is great dry-fly water, where attractor patterns serve well and reliable mayfly and caddis hatches produce good rises. Most anglers fish the 20-odd-mile reach from Bellevue, through Ketchum, and up to the confluence with the North Fork at the foot of the Boulder Mountains.

The Big Wood River is the premier freestone stream in the Magic Valley Region, despite the fact that much of the river flows through the heart of densely populated Sun Valley.

When you drive up the Wood River Valley, you will be struck by the preponderance of private property and you'll begin to wonder about access. Luckily, the Big Wood is legally defined as a navigable river, meaning that so long as you stay within the mean high water line of the river bed, you are not trespassing. Hence, anglers can access the river from the bridges along Hwy. 75 and from any of the eight or so other bridges. Then you need only fish your way up or down the river channel. Many landowners will allow passage to the river as well, so long as anglers take the time to ask, and there are several public access sites.

The Big Wood offers some exceptional hatches, one of the best being a green drake emergence that occurs during late June and early July—a time when the river typically runs high and unfishable due to snow-melt in the mountains upstream. Every once in a while, the climate gods will grant enough of a reprieve that fly anglers can fish over the drake hatch, so if you're in the area during the first week of July, check it out. Even when the water is fairly high, you might find trout sipping the big drakes along the shorelines and in back-eddies.

As soon as the water drops after run-off, hatches of blue-winged olives (*Baetis*) and pale morning duns (*Ephemerella*)—along with some intense caddis hatches—will provide the surface action. The mayflies hatch mid-morning; the caddis hatch both morning and evening. On occasion I've seen some good PMD hatches right at dusk, these usually taking place following 95 degree days. Golden stoneflies and little yellow stoneflies (yellow Sallies) occur during July and August, but neither hatch is a big production.

Two more good mayfly hatches occur during late summer, the first being the Tricos, whose morning hatch/spinner falls create some very challenging fishing on certain stretches of the river. Tricos start winding down by early September when the red quill's begin their emergence. The hatch will last a week or two and although they never hatch in dense numbers, these large mayflies (size 12) get the attention of the trout.

Tiny blue-winged olives return in September, often hatching in large numbers around midday. Thereafter, a few large fall caddis (*Dicosmoecus*) can be found fluttering about during the day and a like imitation will take trout into October.

The Big Wood is open during the winter as well (catch-and-release only) and nymph anglers can do very well between November and March. The river is closed from the end of March until Memorial Day to protect spawning trout.

The myriad access sites to the Big Wood River are identified and shown on a publication titled *Wood River Valley Fishing and Hiking Map & Guide*. To obtain a copy, check with the visitor's bureau in Ketchum, the IDFG, or the Blaine County Recreation District (208/788-2117).

Bear Tracks Preserve, Little Wood River

If hunting big brown trout is your game, then plan a spring or fall visit to Beartracks Preserve on the Little Wood River south of Carey. This section of the Little Wood flows through broken lava fields directly adjacent to Hwy. 93, yet most of the water is out of sight from the road.

In reality, this section of the Little Wood carries mostly Silver Creek waters during the irrigation season, when all or most of the water from the river is diverted. The river channel above the Silver Creek confluence goes completely dry. During peak fishing periods of spring and fall, the river runs quiet and low, its banks lined with lava boulders, dense grasses

Beartracks Preserve on the Little Wood River offers early and late season chances at trophy brown trout.

easy driving and parking. Several rough dirt spurs lead down to the river in places where the old highway bed swings away from the channel (namely on the upstream end).

Some good fishing can be found both above and below the four-mile-long preserve as well. Preacher Bridge, several miles upstream, offers access to some good water at a state recreation site and the remaining 15 miles down to the outskirts of Richfield can be good at times also.

Little Wood Reservoir/Fish Creek Reservoir/Lava Lake

Located on the Little Wood River north of Carey, 600-acre Little Wood Reservoir offers fair fishing for small wild brook trout and planted rainbows. The reservoir offers a nice campground and is located within easy reach of Beartracks if you're looking for a place to camp while fishing the preserve. Look for the signed turnoff just north of Carey.

Nearby Fish Creek Reservoir offers similar fishing for brookies and rainbows. A little farther east on Highway 20, you will find either a lake, pond, or meadow (depending on how dry the climate has been recently) called Lava Lake. When water levels cooperate, the rainbows here can reach 16 inches or more.

Magic Reservoir

At full pool, Magic Reservoir covers an impressive 3,700 surface acres. It stretches five miles in length and reaches depths of 120 feet. Obviously Magic is a big reservoir, but it is also a fertile one, capable of growing trout to impressive sizes in short order.

The key is good water supply and when two or three good water years arrive back-to-back, fly anglers can hook rainbows of four and five pounds, sometimes larger, and brown trout of similar size. Magic Reservoir was overlooked by most fly anglers for many years, but float tubes and pontoon boats are becoming a more common sight these days.

and willows. Stonefly patterns can take fish on top during late spring/early summer and when hoppers are abundant, early September can be good; otherwise, most folks wait until late September and October to pursue 14- to 20-plus-inch browns on streamers and nymphs, along with mouse patterns and large dry-flies. Some hefty rainbows inhabit these waters as well.

The preserve, which is open to catch-and-release, fly-angling-only, was donated by John and Byra Hemingway to the State of Idaho. The preserve is named after Taylor "Beartracks" Williams, who apparently invented the Renegade (a popular Idaho fly) while living in Sun Valley during the 1930s.

To access Beartracks Preserve, follow Hwy. 93 south from Carey about 13 miles. Watch for signs announcing the preserve. Both entrances (one at each end of the preserve) are rather crude gravel affairs, but a length of old paved highway runs parallel to the river, providing both

Magic Reservoir.

GREG THOMAS

Magic Reservoir brown trout.

the entire west shoreline. You can camp along the shore or at Lava Point Campground, which occupies a narrow peninsula about midway up the west bank. Resorts are located on both sides of the reservoir (West Magic and East Magic).

Little Camas Reservoir

Little Camas Reservoir lies just north of Hwy. 20 a few miles past the turnoff to Anderson Ranch Dam and the South Fork Boise. During periods of good water supply, this 1,300-acre, irrigation-storage reservoir can produce good fishing for fat rainbows that typically range from 12 to 18 inches. During a good year, trout over 20 inches are available.

Little Camas thaws by early to mid-May and Dave Tucker, a commercial fly tier from Kuna, recommends wade-fishing along the shoreline shallows during May and June. *Callibaetis* mayflies emerge early here, beginning during May; a sparse but fishable damsel emergence begins in June. Throughout the season, Chironomids emerge in strong numbers, including some dense hatches of large midges. Tucker cautions wading anglers to be wary of the creek channels that drop off to surprising depths.

Oriented north to south, Little Camas is about three miles long, but less than a mile wide in most places. It is shallow throughout. The south end of the reservoir abuts Highway 20. About half of the reservoir lies on Forest Service land, so plenty of rough camping is available, especially on the north end. Forest Service Road 160 turns north off the highway just west of the reservoir and heads 2.5 miles to the boat launch.

Mormon Reservoir

Though not exactly a fly-angling destination, sprawling Mormon Reservoir nonetheless offers a chance for large rainbows (up to 10 pounds) during the heat of summer when the fish congregate around springs in this 2,000-plus-acre impoundment's westernmost arm. You will need a boat to make the long trip back to the springs. The launch is on the north shore and is accessed via Mormon Reservoir Road south of Fairfield.

Baker Lake

This mountain lake, situated near Galena Summit northwest of Ketchum, is notable for the fact that it receives plants of golden trout by the IDFG. Typically these fish are small, like golden trout in many other high lakes, but they are exquisite in color and well worth the short hike up to the lake. Some large cutthroat inhabit the lake as well or at least that was the set-up last time I visited Baker Lake in 1994. Be sure to call IDFG for current conditions. Follow Hwy. 75 through Sun Valley toward Galena Summit and turn left on FR 162 (Baker Creek Road). Follow this road up to the trailhead and walk a steep mile to get to the lake.

Some of the best fly fishing for rainbows is found in the shallows along the southwest shore where good access is provided by a network of gravel roads. During high-water years, float-tube fishing can be good in both the Big Wood arm and the Camas Creek arm on the reservoir's north end as well as in and near the Narrows leading up to that end . If you're using a boat, bear in mind that the boat ramps at this end of the reservoir are high and dry (and unusable) during low-water periods.

Brown trout anglers should pay special attention to the tailwater below Magic Reservoir Dam. Again, when water levels are good for a couple years, some nice browns reside in the river below the reservoir. Other good places to hunt brown trout include the rocky eastern shoreline, where a deep-fished leech pattern, Woolly Bugger or streamer may do the trick. Late fall is typically the best brown trout time, while rainbow fishing is most productive between May and July and again during the fall. Magic Reservoir also has yellow perch and every once in while you'll connect with a big one.

The north end of Magic Reservoir lies immediately south of Hwy. 20 to the west of Hwy. 75. The two high-water boat ramps (Moonstone and Hot Springs landings) are located here. To reach the rest of the reservoir, take Hwy. 75 north from Shoshone or south from Hwy. 20. A few miles south of Hwy. 20 on Hwy. 75 you will find East Magic Reservoir Road, which leads to the east shore. Another six miles or so south on Hwy. 75 takes you to West Magic Reservoir Road, which accesses the dam and

Little Camas Reservoir.

Golden trout from Baker Lake.

Baker Lake near Galena Summit is one of the few places in the West where a one-mile hike allows you the chance to catch golden trout.

South Fork Boise River (above Anderson Ranch Reservoir)

Certainly the South Fork below Anderson Ranch Dam is the region's top stream fishery and one of the best in the Northwest. In addition, the South Fork above the reservoir offers some good pocket-water fishing, both in the river itself and, better yet, in several productive tributaries.

The upper South Fork is heavily stocked with put-and-take rainbows, although some nice wild trout reside in the 12-mile artificials-only stretch from Beaver Creek up to Big Smokey Creek. Big Smokey and Little Smokey are the best tributaries while the shorter feeders like Willow Creek offer good fishing as well. Lime Creek, a tributary to Anderson Ranch Reservoir, is a pleasant stream to hike and fish. Lime Creek enters the reservoir's east side along Forest Route 61.

Route 61, in fact, accesses the upper South Fork and its tributaries. Follow Hwy. 20 north from Interstate 80, past the turnoff to Anderson Ranch Dam. Turn north off Hwy. 20 on either Louse Creek Road or High Prairie Road. These will converge to form Route 61, which winds its way up the east edge of the reservoir, eventually reaching the old mining town of Featherville. The pavement ends at Featherville and from there Forest Service Road 227 heads east up the South Fork.

You can also take a lengthy, but scenic route to the South Fork and the two Smokey Creeks by heading west out of Ketchum on Warm Springs Road. This road veers to the left (northwest) across the street from Silver Creek Outfitters on the north end of downtown Ketchum. After the pavement ends, you can settle in for a long and typically bumpy ride up and over Dollarhide Summit below 9,300-foot Dollarhide Peak. Typically the summit is free of snow by late June, but check with the ranger station in Ketchum before venturing out for a June or early July trip to the South Fork headwaters region.

Once you cross Dollarhide Summit, the road will swing to the south, following Carrie Creek down to Little Smokey Creek. Forest Service Road 227 continues downstream on Little Smokey Creek while FR 015 turns left and explores the creek's lovely upper reaches. At the confluence of Little Smokey and Big Smokey creeks, you can take FR 085 north a short distance to Canyon Campground. From there you must strap on the hiking boots, for walk-in-only is the rule on the majority of this fine fly-fishing water. As you might expect, the fishing improves as you put a few miles behind you.

At the junction where FR 227 meets FR 085, a third road, FR 012, climbs up towards the headwaters of the South Fork. FR 227 continues downstream, passing other fishable tributaries on its way to Featherville. Numerous campgrounds are provided along the river and these get plenty of use during the summer.

Hagerman Wildlife Management Area (HWMA)

Riley Creek flows through the Hagerman Wildlife Management Area and offers fair to good fishing for planted rainbow trout that average six to 12 inches, with a few fish to three or four pounds available. Below the hatchery diversion, Riley Creek and Oster Lakes through which it flows are open March 1 through October 31. Above the hatchery, Riley Creek is open all year. Angler use is heavy most of the year, so if you wish to avoid the crowds, fish early or late in the season and avoid weekends. *Baetis* (blue-winged olive) mayflies produce good rises during the spring and *Callibaetis* (speckled-wing dun) hatches occur throughout much of the season. The many ponds on the HWMA offer good fishing for a variety of warm-water species, including some big bluegill along with large-mouth bass, smallmouth bass, pumpkinseed and crappie.

Hagerman Wildlife Management Area is located three miles south of Hagerman on Hwy. 30 (Thousand Springs Scenic Route). Exit I-84 at Bliss and head south on Hwy. 30 or exit the interstate just west of Wendell on Exit 155 and head west on Hagerman Highway until you reach Hwy. 30. Turn left and drive about a mile to the entrance of HWMA. (You can also turn left before you reach the highway and enter the HWMA from the back side—just follow the signs that point to the federal fish hatchery).

Billingsly Creek (Hagerman Valley)

A mile-long reach of Billingsly Creek flows through Donnie McFadden's Billingsly Creek Ranch and for a time provided exceptional spring-creek fishing for rainbows and browns. McFadden says this upper portion of the creek was "the best kept secret in southern Idaho."

Traditionally, McFadden has allowed five rods per day on his property, asking a nominal per-person fee. The rainbows and browns reached several pounds and fed ravenously on strong hatches of mayflies and midges.

Times have changed for Billingsly Creek: The long drought of the 1980s and early 90s coupled with the state's over-appropriation of the available aquifer has led to a 2/3 reduction in flows in Billingsly Creek. The results of this severe reduction in stream flow is predictable: Dense growths of aquatic weeds now choke the creek each summer and elevate water temperatures. Meanwhile, discharges from the myriad commercial trout hatcheries upstream contribute to the creek's elevated nutrient load, compounding the water-quality problem, and causing heavy siltation of the once-clean gravel bottom.

Fish populations are now depressed and the surviving trout are subject to severe pressure from predatory birds including herons, egrets, cormorants, mergansers and pelicans. The preponderance of commercial fish farms originally caused the artificially elevated populations of these birds in Hagerman Valley. To combat the problem, the fish farms now deploy netting over their rearing ponds to keep the birds out. This leaves Billingsly Creek, with its depressed flows, as a primary option for fish-eating birds, which descend on the stream in hordes.

As a result of the problems facing Billingsly Creek, McFadden now discourages fishing pressure on his reach of the creek in an effort to protect the remaining trout.

Wet winters in the mid-1990s, along with improved discharge practices by the hatcheries, leave room for hope. If water levels return to normal, McFadden says the creek could again return to some semblance of its former glory. For now we must wait, watch and hope for the best. Should the creek recover, McFadden will again be happy to share this lovely creek with anglers willing to ask permission and pay a nominal fee. The two-mile reach from McFadden's property boundary at Tupper Grade upstream to the private sections adjacent to Vader Grade is fly-fishing-only. The public reach below is managed for general regulations

Below McFadden's property, Billingsly Creek flows through another private reach before entering the public access section. This lower access area lies just east of Hagerman: At the north end of town, Hwy. 30 enters a gentle S-curve. As you swing through the curves from either direction, watch for the signs announcing public access. Follow these signs, which will lead you east on Road 1050 East. 1050 East will end at a T-intersection where you will turn left. Follow the road around the corner to the bridge that crosses Billingsly Creek. Limited parking is available on the bend in the road before you reach the creek and at a couple of narrow pullouts at the bridge. From the bridge you can fish downstream. Another access is through Rock Lodge a few hundred yards upstream from the Hwy. 30 bridge on Billingsly Creek.

Dave Tucker, a well-known commercial fly tier and former fly shop owner from Kuna, recommends tiny dry-flies on light tippets and a downstream presentation. He notes that even during hatches of PMD, blue-winged olive and speckled-wing dun mayflies, a tiny Griffith's Gnat or similar pattern will often out-fish flies that represent the emerging insects.

The lower end of Billingsly Creek has suffered from the same problems affecting the reaches upstream. On the public-access section, the trout face the additional pressure from moderate to heavy angler use. Still, early-season fishing for mostly small trout is available and should improve as water levels return to normal.

Incidentally, Dave Tucker recommends that fly anglers in the Hagerman Valley take the time to seek permission to explore the many small creeks, canals, and drainage ditches in the area because escaped trout from the numerous hatcheries inhabit many of these waters and

At one time, Billingsly Creek Ranch boasted of the best-kept fishing secret in southern Idaho. Recent water quality and quantity problems, however, have prompted owner Don McFadden to put a hold on access until the stream recovers. Given its storied past, this creek is well worth the effort should the fishery recover to former levels.

can provide excellent fishing. In addition, several major streams enter the Snake River in this region and these can provide good fishing in an uncrowded environment for those willing to do some exploring. These include Salmon Falls Creek and the Malad River.

Jarbridge River

If you are looking for a remote river in a wild desert canyon, look no further than the Jarbridge, whose seldom-fished waters contain native red-band trout, along with a few bull trout and whitefish. For the most part, you won't want to travel this remote corner of southern Idaho without two spare tires, extra gas, lots of water and all the usual emergency equipment. Also obtain a good map from the BLM.

The other items you'll need include a good pair of hiking boots and a willingness to use them, for the best reaches of the Jarbridge require a bit of work. If indeed you are willing to take two or three days to explore the river, you'll find good fishing for wild redbands in the six- to 12-inch range with an occasional 14- to 18-inch trout. The entire Idaho portion of the river offers good fishing, but the section in Nevada is usually better (be sure to obtain a Nevada license). Fishing begins in mid-June, after spring run-off subsides; cooler weather in autumn offers excellent fishing as well.

The easiest access to the Jarbridge is from Murphy Hot Springs a few miles north of the Nevada border. Follow Hwy. 93 south out of Twin Falls until you reach the turnoff for Salmon Falls Creek Dam (Three Creeks Road) follow this road west, past the dam, past Cedar Creek Reservoir, past the headwaters of the East Fork Bruneau, and down to Murphy Hot Springs. From there you can hike the canyon. With a good 4X4, you can drive rough back roads both in Idaho and Nevada and then hike the river banks. The farther you get from Murphy Hot Springs, the fewer people you will encounter.

Bruneau River

Another of the remote desert trout streams of southwest Idaho, the Bruneau can offer good summer and fall fishing for native redband trout up to 14 inches. This is rugged, remote canyon country where you will need a four-wheel-drive vehicle and good BLM maps (and a willingness to walk). Most of the river flows through a steep canyon and very few roads actually reach the river. The best fishing for trout is from the confluence of the Bruneau's east and west forks upstream (on both forks). Below the confluence of the forks, smallmouth become increasingly common. The eight-mile reach from Hot Springs down to C.J. Strike Reservoir is open all year. Hwy. 51 out of Mountain Home will take you south, across the Snake River, to the tiny town of Bruneau. From there, Hot Springs Road (or Hot Creek Road west of town) will take you south to Hot Springs. From there, refer to a good BLM map for approaches to the river. To explore the upper reaches, follow Hwy. 51 south towards Grasmere and again refer to BLM maps. The East Fork Bruneau is accessed via Clover/Three Creeks Road south of Saylor Creek Air Force Range (again, don't venture out without a good BLM map).

Sublett Reservoir

One-hundred-acre Sublett Reservoir offers planted rainbows, wild cutthroat and wild brown trout. During good water years, the fish can grow large in this fertile reservoir. This is good float-tube water. The reservoir is located on the eastern edge of the Magic Valley Region, southeast of Burley. Access is easy. Just follow I-84 past Burley and continue on the freeway as it swings south on its way to Utah (remember to turn south when you see the signs for Utah rather than continuing on I-86 toward Pocatello). Watch the mileposts and when you reach Exit 245, follow Sublett Road about 10 miles up to the reservoir. You will find diminutive Sublett Campground due east of the reservoir's east arm on Forest Service Road 583 and there are plenty of rough campsites in the area. Also, the little creeks that drain the Sublett Mountains can offer some fun fishing for small but eager trout.

SOUTHWEST & SALMON REGIONS

Idaho's southwest and Salmon regions, by way of their respective boundaries, feature a splendid variety of both landscapes and fisheries. The most remote waters in Idaho are found in two extremes in this region: The desert streams of extreme southwestern Idaho and the highland lakes and creeks of the central Idaho mountains.

The Salmon River cuts a path across the center of Idaho: Its source is the Sawtooth Valley, where streams draining the east side of the Sawtooth Range and the west side of the White Cloud Peaks combine their waters to form a gliding gravel-bottom river that meanders its way through the broad valley, flowing north, east, and then north again after combining with the East Fork Salmon. Highway 93 picks up the river at Challis and then parallels it past the town of Salmon, where the now-mighty river swings westerly on its journey all the way across Idaho.

Strengthened further by the famed Middle Fork and the South Fork, along with countless smaller tributaries, the Salmon forges a massive presence upon reaching Riggins and then White Bird along Route 95 on the western edge of the state. Finally, after surging through one last long and lonely reach below Pine Bar, the Salmon relinquishes its waters to the Snake River at Hells Canyon.

In the heart of central Idaho—in the land drained by the Salmon River watershed—the adventuresome angler will find solitude aplenty. The history-conscious angler will find a land once roamed by the great Nez Perce; a land that nearly brought the Lewis & Clark expedition to its knees; a land that offered temporary escape for the tiny band of Sheepeaters, who in 1879, held the U.S. cavalry at bay on several occasions before finally agreeing to abandon their wilderness home for a life on the reservation.

To the south of the Salmon River country, the southwest region boasts of one of the top trout fisheries in the West, the South Fork of the Boise River below Anderson Dam. This tailwater fishery, once a quietly productive rainbow river for local fly anglers, has gained national prominence: The South Fork is defined by clear, cold flows, abundant hatches, large trout, and spectacular canyon landscape.

Southwestern Idaho is also one of the first regions in the West where fly anglers embraced the use of "belly boats" or float tubes for stillwater fishing. Reservoirs such as Sagehen, Horsethief and Sheep Creek (the latter located in Nevada on the Duck Valley Indian Reservation) traditionally offer quality fishing for big rainbows and it was on such waters where Ruel Stayner, George Biggs, Darrell Grim, Mick Miller, Tex Meeks, Ken Magee, Marv Taylor and other local float-tubers developed many effective stillwater flies, some of which have gained national popularity. Taylor records these patterns in his 1979 book, *Float Tubes, Fly Rods & Other Essays*.

Float-tube waters do in fact abound in the western part of Idaho. The southwest region offers not only the productive reservoirs that hosted the area's pioneering float-tubers, but also a series of high lakes in the McCall area that are set aside for fly angling and where a tube-packing fly rodder might find both large trout and some peace and quiet. Along the Snake River, warm-water enthusiasts can ply small ponds, sloughs and backwaters for largemouth and smallmouth bass, crappie and bluegill.

Geographically, the southwest region, combined with the Salmon region to the east, covers a substantial chunk of the state. No doubt this huge area offers its blue-ribbon waters such as the South Fork Boise. More numerous are exceptional fisheries that have either escaped the prying eyes of the fly angling media (e.g. Little Payette Lake) or are simply too remote to be heavily trampled by anglers, as is the case with much of the Salmon River and its forks.

A South Fork Boise River rainbow that fell for a Beadhead Pheasant Tail Nymph during the winter.

SOUTHWEST REGION, NORTH HALF

Little Payette Lake

Averaging around 1,450 acres, Little Payette Lake is managed as a fly/artificial-lure-only trophy trout fishery for rainbows that reach 20 inches or more. Current regulations offer a two-fish limit, but any trout retained must be 20 inches or over. A good percentage of the trout are longer than 14 inches with quite a few in the 16- to 18-inch category. The lake also supports smallmouth bass, with an occasional big one, and kokanee (25-fish limit on the kokanee).

To reach Little Payette Lake, about half of which is surrounded by private property, leave McCall's main intersection (where Route 55 turns left to head up to New Meadows) on Lick Creek Road. If you are arriving from the south on Hwy. 55, just go straight through the intersection rather than following 55 as it turns left to swing through town. Watch for the signs to Ponderosa State Park and follow these as you swing around to the right on Pine Street and then to the left on Hemlock Street. Take a left at Davis Street (still following the signs for Ponderosa Park) and proceed one half mile along Davis Avenue before turning right on Lick Creek Road. Go 2.5 miles to Y-intersection where you will take the right fork. The pavement ends within a half mile and from there you are just a short drive over nasty gravel washboards to the lake's north shore.

A good summer *Callibaetis* hatch provides dry-fly action when the wind stays down and the lake harbors good populations of damsels, Chironomids and other trout foods. The lake opens on Memorial Day weekend and remains open until the end of November. Autumn fishing can be excellent. This is fine float-tube water, but owing to the lake's size, a canoe or pram will help if you like to explore.

Lake Fork Creek

A beautiful little mountain stream, Lake Fork Creek feeds Little Payette Lake. The lake's rainbows run up into the creek so some surprisingly large trout are available to anglers who can fish with a fair degree of stealth over the creek's gin-clear waters.

A short section of the stream flows along the gravel road. Above this section, the creek winds away from the road and through some private property. Anglers willing to hike-in to the reach below Brown's Pond will find the trout less pressured. Check with the fly shop in McCall for directions (Lick Creek Outfitters).

South Fork Salmon River and Tributaries

The South Fork Salmon is a remote highland river originating in the Salmon River Mountains east of the town of Cascade in Valley County. From its headwaters south of Warm Lake, the South Fork flows for many miles through diverse and wild landscapes before finally entering the main Salmon at Mackay Bar. The last ten miles of the South Fork flow through the River of No Return Wilderness.

Idaho's B-run steelhead—the same strain found in the Clearwater River—spawn in the South Fork in numbers too limited to allow for a sport season (check current regulations, however). Still, the South Fork does offer good fishing for wild cutthroat and rainbows, the former being afforded full protection under no-harvest rules. The entire river is catch-and-release up to the mouth of the Secesh River.

The Secesh itself, along with the East Fork of the South Fork Salmon and numerous other tributaries offer good trout fishing as well, especially when you get away from the Forest Service roads that access the region.

The South Fork and its tributaries are characterized by extensive pocket water interrupted in turn by gliding runs, shallow riffles, and elegant bubble-shot pools. Some meandering meadow sections are available on certain tribs. Caddis abound in these waters and stoneflies hatch in rather sparse numbers throughout the summer. Fast-water mayflies are common, as are many terrestrial insects, including hoppers. Search out deserted sections of stream on the South Fork or its feeders and you will find eager trout. Most don't grow large, but the occasional 14- to 20-inch fish provides ample room for anticipation.

Access to the South Fork and many of its tributaries is primarily by lengthy drives on Forest Service roads of all descriptions. The only easy access to the upper river lies east of Cascade on Warm Lake Road (the same road that leads to Horsethief Reservoir). Just north of the Payette River on the north edge of town, Warm Lake Road heads east from the highway and shoots across the valley before heading up into the national forest. As I recall, the river is 25 miles up this road (Forest Route 22).

Once you cross the river, Forest Service Road 474 leads north and south along the east bank. Going south for several miles, FR 474 deteriorates to rough gravel and dirt before finally ending. To the north, FR 474/674 follows the river for some 30 miles to the junction with Forest Route 48 (Lick Creek Road out of McCall). Turn east on FR 48 and follow the East Fork of the South Fork Salmon all the way to its headwaters near Murphy Peak and Monumental Summit. Turn west on 48 and follow the lower Secesh River for five miles before heading down Lick Creek and eventually reaching McCall. From the confluence of the South Fork and the Secesh, FR 674 heads down the South Fork for about three miles. Here the road ends and the trail begins, following a nine-mile roadless reach of the river.

The last drive-in access to the South Fork is via Warren Wagon Road (FR 21/340) which leads past Upper Payette Lake, up Summit Creek, down Secesh Meadows, up to Warren, and finally down to the South Fork Guard Station and Shiefer Campground. If that sounds to you like a long drive, you're right: The route covers nearly 50 miles.

Little Salmon River

The Little Salmon River is known primarily for its spring steelhead fishing. As of this writing, the river is open to steelhead angling from its mouth up to the Hwy. 95 bridge near Smokey Boulder Road, but be sure to check current regulations.

The falls near Round Valley Creek block passage of anadromous fish to the upper reaches of the Little Salmon. Above Round Valley Creek, the river meanders in wide curves through Meadows Valley. The water looks good and does offer some fishing for rainbows, brook trout, and cutthroat, but virtually all the land in the meadow is private property. For the most part, you'll need to seek permission if you wish to explore the Little Salmon in its meadow reaches.

Below the meadows, trout fishing can be decent after the midsummer opener. Check current regulations for season dates. Hwy. 95 follows the Little Salmon from New Meadows north to the river's confluence with the Salmon at Riggins.

The Rapid River, a major tributary to the Little Salmon, offers fairly secluded trout fishing in its upper reaches (well above the hatchery). This is walk-in-only water. The Payette National Forest map shows the myriad trails into the river.

High Lakes of the Payette/South Fork Salmon Drainage

The Payette and South Fork drainages feature numerous fishable high mountain lakes. As of last count, eight of these lakes are managed as trophy trout fisheries where only barbless flies and lures are allowed and where any trout less than 20 inches in length must be released. During any given year, at least one, and usually several, of these lakes will offer cutthroat or rainbows that can exceed 20 inches, with 14- to 18-inch trout being common. For specific directions, consult the Payette and Boise National Forest Maps and the USGS topo maps (and call Payette National Forest headquarters in McCall).

The eight trophy lakes are as follows: Blackwell Lake and Crystal Lake are located north of Little Payette Lake not far from McCall. Lake

Rock Lake is northeast from Upper Payette Lake on the Summit Creek drainage. Louie Lake is located just south of Boulder Meadows Reservoir a few miles southeast of Little Payette Lake. Brush Lake lies west of Lick Creek Summit, the trail being located on FR 432 off Route 21 south of Upper Payette Lake. Tule Lake sits just southwest of Warm Lake in the Boise National Forest northwest of Cascade, and Long Lake is accessed via the Telephone Ridge Trail several miles south of Warm Lake. Finally, Lake Serene is found west of Hard Creek Guard Station (near Hazard Lakes) on FR 257 north by northeast of New Meadows.

Upper Payette Lake/Upper North Fork Payette River

A put-and-take fishery for hatchery rainbows and some brook trout, Upper Payette is located north of McCall along Forest Route 21, the Warren Wagon Road. The river between Upper Payette Lake and Payette Lake offers easy-access fishing for planted rainbows, along with a few cutthroat and brook trout. Splake were introduced a few years ago.

Middle North Fork Payette River

Below McCall, the Middle North Fork Payette flows through private lands in Long Valley before entering Cascade Reservoir. The river contains some decent wild rainbows along with hatchery stocks, but access is difficult. I've accessed the river near the bridge on Smiley Lane, which turns off Hwy. 55 south of McCall and West Mountain Road runs above the west bank. Ask permission to cross private lands and check with the IDFG in McCall for further access suggestions.

Sagehen Reservoir

A rainbow trout reservoir located among lush coniferous forest in the Boise National Forest south of Cascade Reservoir, Sagehen is capable of producing good-sized fish. However, the reservoir is heavily fished and does not currently have the benefit of any special regulations.

Still rainbows to 16 inches are available during good years and the reservoir is good float-tube water, being protected from the wind to a degree because of the surrounding ridges. The water remains clear for most of the season and May and June offer good damsel emergences. *Callibaetis* mayflies and other trout foods common to Western reservoirs all reside in the lake in fairly good numbers.

To reach Sagehen Reservoir, drive north out of Boise on Hwy. 55 to the town of Smiths Ferry. After passing through town, look for Cougar Mountain Lodge on the right. The road to Sagehen Reservoir begins across the highway from the lodge and climbs steeply before leveling off and winding and bumping its way some 12 miles to the reservoir (watch out for log trucks!). Signs will keep you headed in the right direction. The reservoir is encircled by a paved road that accesses five campgrounds.

Horsethief Reservoir

This scenic and productive, 1,270-acre reservoir occupies a shallow basin in the forested hills east of the town of Cascade. Rainbows are the usual fare at Horsethief, but brook trout are present, as are stocked brown trout. Despite being a popular put-and-take fishery with no special regulations, Horsethief is productive enough to produce some decent trout during good years. The reservoir is good float-tube water.

To reach Horsethief, follow Hwy. 55 north from Boise or south from McCall to the town of Cascade at the southern end of Cascade Reservoir. Just north of the Payette River bridge at Cascade, turn east on Warm Lake Road and follow the pavement about six miles to the Horsethief Reservoir Road (gravel), which heads south to the reservoir. Ample camp space is available.

Horsethief Reservoir has long been a favorite among southwest Idaho float-tubers.

Brundage Reservoir

Brundage Reservoir is located in the Payette National Forest north by northwest of McCall. The reservoir is an elongated affair of more than a mile in length and features a two-trout bag with a slot limit that requires release of all trout between 12 and 20 inches. Such regulations might suggest a trophy-type fishery, but the majority of the larger trout in Brundage fall within the lower end of that slot range with rainbows more than 15 inches being uncommon.

Still Brundage is rarely crowded and offers enjoyable float tube and boat fishing, along with some productive shoreline angling, especially at its upper end early and late in the season. Attractor wet-flies and streamers—Carey Specials, Woolly Buggers, Sheep Creek Specials, Stayner Ducktails, etc—will suffice much of the time. A good *Callibaetis* hatch offers reliable dry-fly fishing during the summer, at least when the wind stays down.

To reach Brundage Reservoir follow Hwy. 55 northeast from McCall (or Hwy. 95 if you are coming from the north or southwest). Between McCall and New Meadows you will wind over a pass through the mountains, near the top of which is the turnoff for Brundage Mountain Ski Resort. Follow this road north. Four miles of pavement will take you to the ski resort, but continue up the hill on a good gravel road for another three miles where you will find a Y-intersection. The right fork leads about a mile over a rough gravel road to Brundage Reservoir. No campgrounds, but lots of good unimproved campsites.

The road to Brundage follows the southeast edge of the reservoir and then winds its way up toward Granite Lake (deteriorating along the way). Better still are the Hazard Lakes to the north of Brundage. To reach these productive mountain lakes continue on FR 257 past the Brundage Reservoir turnoff and proceed approximately 15 miles up to Hazard Lake Campground. From here you can fish Big Hazard Lake, Hazard Lake (no motors) and Upper Hazard Lake (a hike-in lake) along with several other small lakes. Check with Payette National Forest for road and trail conditions.

Deadwood Reservoir

A put-and-take reservoir in Valley County on Deadwood River southeast of Cascade. Deadwood is stocked with cutthroat and rainbow trout along with fall chinook salmon, Atlantic salmon and kokanee. The fish range from 10 to 16 inches in this 2,700-acre mountain reservoir. Access is by Scott Mountain Road about four miles past Danskin take-out on the South Fork Payette River.

The author fishes Brundage Reservoir, where 10- to 18-inch rainbows thrive in a quiet setting north of McCall.

Sulphur Creek

One of several catch-and-release streams for native cutthroat in the region, Sulphur Creek flows almost entirely through a corner of the Frank Church River of No Return Wilderness and into the Middle Fork of the Salmon River. Virtually the entire creek is hike-in only. Native cutthroat and bull trout inhabit the creek, and steelhead and fall chinook traditionally spawn here. The cutthroat, which are the main attraction during the fishable season from late July through October, can reach 16 or more inches in length. Best access for this lightly fished mountain stream is from the Boundary Creek Float-boat Launch on the Middle Fork of the Salmon

Bear Valley Creek

Other Middle Fork tributary creeks in the area offer equally productive fishing for cutthroat, with the least accessible waters offering the highest quality experience. These include wilderness streams such as Pistol Creek, Indian Creek, Rapid River and Camas Creek.

Similar to Sulphur Creek in its offerings, Bear Valley Creek is more accessible but not as heavily fished. The canyon section below Fir Creek Campground is best for native cutthroat trout. The creek also offers brook trout, especially in its upper reaches. Bear Valley Road turns to the west off Route 21 just a few miles before 21 makes its swing from a northeasterly direction to a southeasterly direction north of the Sawtooth Recreation Area.

Several other non-wilderness-area creeks offer similar opportunities for small-stream cutthroat angling, including Elk Creek, Clear Creek and numerous others. Consult River of No Return Wilderness map or Boise National Forest map.

South Fork Payette River

Popular with white-water enthusiasts, the beautiful, 60-mile-long South Fork Payette is also a good trout stream with native rainbows that commonly range from nine to 13 inches. From the Deadwood River confluence to the South Fork's mouth, the river is managed for wild trout; same for the upper section above 10-Mile Bridge (above Lowman). The best section is from Deadwood River down to Danskin take-out.

This is a predominantly caddis-stonefly stream. Giant stoneflies hatch early in the summer, typically before all of the run-off has subsided. Strong evening caddis hatches can create good rises and attractor dry-flies will do the job during the day. Mid-July through early August typically brings an end to the run-off and the fishing remains productive into October.

Much of the South Fork is accessible from the road, although in places anglers must scramble down steep embankments. Float boats can be used to access some areas as well. The uppermost river, above Grandjean Campground, flows from the high crags of the Sawtooth Wilderness and is hike-in only.

The Payette River offers fair to good dry-fly fishing for small trout during summer and fall for those willing to scramble the rip-rap highway embankments.

To reach the South Fork you can choose two routes. For the lower river, follow Hwy. 55 north from Boise until you reach the little wide spot called Banks, where a store/restaurant overlooks the North Fork Payette River. Just past the store is the turnoff for the South Fork. The other option is Route 21 from Boise north to Lowman and east/northeast along the river as far as Grandjean Road. To reach the Deadwood River area proceed west out of Lowman to White water Campground.

Middle Fork Payette River

Joining the South Fork Payette about eight miles east of Banks, the Middle Fork offers wild and stocked rainbow trout, with the highest quality fishery being along the roadless section upstream from Boiling Springs Campground (a section which is not stocked). The roadless area offers access by trail in sections and by bushwhacking in others. Best access sites for the roadless section are Boiling Springs Ranger Station and Silver Creek Lookout. Consult the Boise National Forest for road and trail conditions and for specific directions.

North Fork Payette River

Despite flowing along Hwy. 55 for much of its length, the North Fork Payette offers good fishing for small rainbows amidst some of the state's most awesome white water. Steep climbs down riprap highway embankments are typical for North Fork anglers, but the river's rainbows generally prove to be eager risers and are equally responsive to streamers and nymphs.

The section from Cascade to Carbarton Bridge is away from the highway and is flotable. Below the bridge are some serious rapids before the river broadens to a wide, barren frog-water expanse as its passes through Smiths Ferry. Below Smiths Ferry, the river again picks up steam, forming some truly awesome rapids that only the most experienced white-water enthusiasts dare try. The roadside edge of these extensive white water sections offers rip-rap fishing for those willing to scramble down the embankment. Forget waders and opt for shoes or boots that will grip the big rocks forming the roadbed.

A good stonefly hatch (*Pteronarcys*) appears between Mother's Day and Memorial Day, although spring/early summer releases from Cascade Reservoir usually make the river high and somewhat off-color—but not necessarily unfishable—during this time. Between late July and October the North Fork typically remains fishable.

Weiser River Drainage

The Weiser River is heavily de-watered for extensive agriculture interests in the region and, except for its headwater forks, offers little of interest to fly anglers. The Little Weiser, East Fork Weiser, Middle Fork Weiser and West Fork Weiser offer fair small-stream fishing for mostly small redband and brook trout. Also, bull trout cling to existence in these waters.

All of these tributaries originate in the Payette National Forest, so access is good. Three of the forks drain the West Mountains along the Adams/Valley County line east of Council and Cambridge. Best access to the west slope of the West Mountains is from Hwy. 95 in the vicinity of Council. Check the Payette National Forest map for specifics.

Several irrigation storage reservoirs in the Weiser Valley area offer good warm-water fishing along with sometimes-good trout fishing. These include Mann Creek Reservoir, Ben Ross Reservoir and Crane Creek Reservoir. During summer, substantial drawdowns are the rule on these reservoirs.

SOUTHWEST REGION, SOUTH HALF

South Fork Boise River

The South Fork is one of the state's top freestone rivers, offering large, wild rainbows in a spectacular canyon setting. The river's productivity results from the cold, fertile outflows of Anderson Ranch Dam. Hatches are predictable and many offer exceptional dry-fly fishing, among them the stonefly hatch, pink Cahill hatch and various caddis emergences.

The South Fork Boise flows through a stunning semi-arid canyon below Anderson Ranch Reservoir.

Forrest Maxwell fishes the shadows via kick boat on the South Fork Boise.

My first summertime visit to the South Fork just happened to coincide perfectly with a tremendous hatch of the little pink Alberts or pink cahills. These elegant little mayflies (*Epeorus albertae*) hatch midday on the South Fork, even under the scorching summer sun. When the hatch came off that day, Forrest Maxwell and I found ourselves in the right place at the right time: In a slow, gentle run up against one bank, we found a pod of 16- to 20-inch rainbows casually sipping away at the little mayflies. They reminded me of Silver Creek 'bows in the way they podded up and chomped away at the surface.

The first of these fish was easy. Our host that day was Dave Tucker, who had earlier given me a couple of his Pink Cahill Parachute patterns. A downstream presentation with a long leader and one of those Parachutes did the trick. I landed a stunning fish of about 18 inches. That was the last fish fooled by the Parachute until I clipped away most of the fly's hackle and wing, in essence making a floating nymph out of the pattern. The second trout rose confidently for my "reduced" version of Tucker's fly and then dashed immediately into a root-wad below.

Hands shaking in excitement, I took the second of Dave's Pink Cahills and clipped away at the wing and hackle. On the first cast, a trout rose toward the fly, then turned away without rising. On subsequent casts, I got two refusals in the form of bulges (where the trout turns away just before rising) and two more follows by trout that backed downstream with the fly for two feet before abandoning any interest in rising.

I went to the fly boxes and selected a light olive *Baetis* Floating Nymph—the same pattern I often use on the Henry's Fork and on Silver Creek and yet here we were on a freestone river. One big trout had moved several feet above the main pod and began feeding against the bank. My first cast rose the fish and hooked it solidly. This latter fact was apparently not to its liking, or so I judged by the way it sprinted immediately to

mid-river, cartwheeled three times in the heavy current, and then broke off on its way to destinations well downstream.

At this point, with a dozen or so fish still devouring mayflies in this little side current, I waved Forrest down to meet me. Between the two of us we rose three or four more of those brutes before the hatch concluded and each fish required every bit as much finesse as rising trout on the flat waters of Idaho's famous spring creeks.

That was the day I became a big fan of the South Fork. This terrific fishery starts at Anderson Ranch Dam, where cold water assures that the river below offers ideal conditions for the resident rainbows. While pods of truly large trout like those Forrest and I encountered are not really the norm, these big rainbows are fairly common and they tend to be most available during good hatches or when lots of hoppers or cicadas are in the drift. The river boasts lots of 12- to 15-inch rainbows and every once in a while a truly remarkable trout makes an appearance: The same day that Forrest and I were fishing that side channel, Dave Tucker was downstream battling a monstrous rainbow in one of the river's deep pools.

What's more, the South Fork is essentially a year-round fishery. During fall and winter, flows are minimized and wading is easy. By December, the major hatches come to an end, but nymphs and streamers will produce throughout the winter. Midge hatches occur just about any day during the winter when temperatures climb above freezing and occasionally these emergences will bring a few trout to the surface. During mid- to late March in most years, *Baetis* mayflies begin to hatch each day. Little brown stoneflies also emerge during mid-March.

The South Fork closes at the end of March and then re-opens Memorial Day weekend. The winter season (Dec. 1 through March) is catch-and-release only. Unfortunately, the river offers a two-fish limit during the general season, but as no fish between 12 and 20 inches may be retained, the prime spawning-age rainbows are protected.

4251

No. 0

GREG THOMAS

The South Fork offers many strong hatches
throughout the season.

During a normal year, when the South Fork re-opens at the end of May, *Baetis* hatches and a few early golden stoneflies and caddis provide some surface activity. During low-water years, stoneflies and caddis may offer strong hatches at the time of the May opener. Otherwise, expect a tremendous caddis hatch to begin around the middle of June and last for two weeks. Blanket hatches of these little gray caddis are not unusual. Towards the end of the caddis hatch, the stoneflies begin, with both salmonflies and golden stones (brown willow flies) sharing the scene. During a typical year, the stonefly hatch will last through mid-July.

The aforementioned pink cahills or pink Alberts begin to hatch sometime during early or mid-July. Typically the hatch remains strong through August, but can last well into the fall. Look for PMDs to accompany the *Epeorus* hatch, especially during the occasional overcast day in late June or early July. *Baetis* hatches return in the fall, along with a strong hatch of craneflies from mid-September through mid-October. A sporadic October caddis emergence is of limited importance most of the time.

Terrestrial insects can be prolific and important, with hoppers and cicadas chief among these. The cicadas are big and black—a size 6 Black Maxwell's Jughead or Tucker Foam Cricket makes an excellent imitation. Ants and beetles are abundant and their imitations can be effective, especially when fished under overhanging brush against the banks.

During a typical year, the water level on the South Fork remains low and stable between September and March (300 to 600 cfs). During this time period, the river is very wadeable. The dam is uncorked at the end of March and flows typically run between 4,000 and 5,000 cfs until the second week in June. Then the flows are cut to around 2,000 or 2,500 cfs for the balance of the summer. Although the water remains clear, these summer flows make wading difficult in many places, so floating the river has become quite popular with fly anglers.

Pontoon boats have become a popular option with fly anglers on the South Fork, but be careful as there are a few tricky spots between Anderson Ranch Dam and Danskin. Drift boats are ideal for this medium-sized river. During the fall, winter and early spring, the river usually gets too low for an easy drift, so wading is the method of choice.

During summer, the 10-plus-mile float from the rough put-in below the dam down to Danskin Bridge is a full-day journey when the fishing is good. For shorter trips, there are two easy launches in between: The first is Village at mile 3, the second is Cow Creek Bridge at mile 9.

The lower 17-mile reach of the South Fork, from Danskin down to Neal Bridge, offers equally productive fishing in a remote canyon setting. Far fewer anglers reach this section because the only access is by boat and the drift is a dangerous one requiring a high degree of skill at the oars of drift boat or raft. Neal Bridge is accessed via Blacks Creek Road (Exit 64) off I-84 southeast of Boise. This float includes many serious rapids and shouldn't be attempted during low flows.

To reach the South Fork from Boise, follow Interstate 84 southeast to Mountain Home and turn north on Hwy. 20. Follow Hwy. 20 north and then east some 20 miles. After climbing over Tollgate Hill, watch for signs announcing Anderson Dam and Fall Creek Recreation Area. Turn left (north) at the signs and follow Anderson Dam Road down into the South Fork Boise River Canyon. From the east, follow Hwy. 20 west from the Sun Valley area. Look for the Anderson Dam turnoff about three miles west of Little Camas Reservoir, whose south shore parallels the highway.

The steep, switchback-laden gravel road down into this impressive canyon can be treacherous during winter. In fact, I'll have nothing to do with this road when any amount of snow or ice enters the picture. Even during summer, the road can prove awfully hard on brakes and radiators.

Once you reach the dam, cross to the north side and turn left. Forest Service Road 113 follows the river for about 10 miles down to Danskin Bridge. Along the way, you will find plenty of nice camping areas on Forest Service land, none of which are improved and none of which require a fee, at least as of this writing.

Flies for the South Fork Boise

As with most top-notch trout streams, the South Fork Boise has inspired its own flock of local patterns. Some were created to match specific hatches or meet specific needs on this unique river. Many of the same flies listed for the South Fork of the Snake will perform well on the South Fork Boise. In addition, the following flies have proven their value on the latter stream (see fly plates and selected dressings):

Tucker Foam Cricket	Cranefly Skater
Pink Cahill	South Fork Caddis, Light
Pink Cahill Parachute	South Fork Caddis, Dark
Pink Compara-dun	Z-lon Midge
Pink CDC Dun	Bead-Head Caddis Larva

Middle Fork Boise River

When I last visited the Middle Fork of the Boise a number of years ago I was met by an elegant and remote freestone river guarded in places by steep canyon walls and shaded by ponderosas, cottonwoods and Douglas firs. Unfortunately, its tumbling pocket waters, glassy pools, and gliding runs were largely home to a mix of put-and-take hatchery trout and diminutive native rainbows.

Forrest Maxwell battles a South Fork rainbow that took an
Elk Hair Caddis during a July evening above Danskin.

Not nearly so famous as the South Fork, the Middle Fork Boise nonetheless offers good fishing in its remote reaches.

Since that time, however, management of the Middle Fork has changed in favor of wild trout and rumors suggest that above its confluence with the North Fork, the Middle Fork of the Boise is fast becoming a first-rate fishery for wild rainbows. Though they tend towards the small size, these trout thrive in classic dry-fly water where caddisflies and stoneflies abound and where a good grasshopper crop makes August and September a pleasant time to visit.

The Middle Fork originates in the Sawtooth Wilderness. Its headwaters, which I have visited more recently, offer good fishing for small but eager trout in a truly beautiful setting. To get there you drive over miles of bumpy gravel up the Middle Fork to the old mining community of Atlanta. Continue a short distance up to the trailhead and have at it. Or you do it the hard way, which I highly recommend: Enter the Sawtooth Wilderness from the Hell Roaring Lake Trailhead and hike up over the pass behind Imogene Lake, then up behind Glen Peak and finally down to the headwaters of the Middle Fork. Throw in a bunch of trout-filled high lakes and you'll need a week to do it right.

After leaving the wilderness, the South Fork swings west on its long journey down to Arrowrock Reservoir. Forest Service Road 268 follows the river for its entire length. To get to the Middle Fork, follow Hwy. 21 east out of Boise and past Lucky Peak Dam. About six miles past the dam, turn right on a well-marked road that winds along the north shore of Lucky Peak Lake and Arrowrock Reservoir on its way up the Middle Fork.

North Fork Boise River

The North Fork Boise also offers good fishing for wild rainbows if you are willing to hike its roadless sections. The first of these runs from the confluence with the Middle Fork up to Forest Service Road 327 (Rabbit Creek Road), which heads east off Hwy. 21 just north of Idaho City.

The second roadless section is upstream, from Deer Park Campground to Johnson Creek Campground. Both of these reaches span about seven miles in length. Another roadless stretch heads for several miles up into the Sawtooth Wilderness and up to the headwaters of the North Fork. Productive tributaries include the walk-in lower half of Crooked River (downstream from FR 384) and Bear River.

C.J. Strike Reservoir

Spanning 7,500 surface acres, C.J. Strike Reservoir backs up the waters of the lower Bruneau River and the Snake River, forming a roughly horseshoe-shaped affair southwest of Mountain Home. Strike Reservoir won't find its way onto anybody's list of blue-ribbon fly-rod waters, but its Bruneau Arm offers some intriguing mixed bag fishing, including an opportunity for large rainbows during early spring and fall. Look for shallow shoal areas or fish the Narrows (east of the dam and west of Cottonwood Campground). Access sites are plentiful off Hwy. 78, which parallels the south shore. Bruneau Narrows Access, Cottonwood Access and Jack's Creek Access offer lots of good water. When the water gets too warm for shallow-water trout fishing, fish rock structures and drop-offs for smallmouth bass, which attain impressive sizes. Easiest access to the Bruneau Arm is from Mountain Home, where you will turn south on Hwy. 51. Follow Hwy. 51 past the town of Bruneau until you reach the Hwy. 78 intersection. Hwy. 78 leads a short distance to the reservoir.

Owyhee River

The Owyhee River flows from northern Nevada through the southwest corner of Idaho and then into Oregon. The Idaho Reach is about as remote a trout stream as you could hope to find and one had better not venture there unless well-prepared to travel in a desert environment where the nearest services are many miles away by dirt roads.

The river and its tributaries follow remote and spectacular canyons carved out over the eons. Resident rainbows and whitefish cling to life, over-summering in scattered pools and fluctuating in population with the drought cycles that dictate life in the Great Basin West.

The Owyhee's major tributaries are even more remote. The South Fork Owyhee and Little Owyhee are difficult to access and are rarely visited by fly anglers; same goes for Battle Creek and Deep Creek. These streams fight the perennial battle against evaporation and drought in the Idaho desert. Their native redband trout evolved here, allowing scant populations to survive drought cycles, waiting to re-populate the river with their progeny when flows stabilize during wet seasons. In any year, trout populations in the Little Owyhee and South Fork Owyhee are sparse and virtually never fished (after all, one could drive from Boise to Yellowstone National Park in less time than it takes to reach these remote streams).

The North Fork Owyhee joins the mainstem in Oregon, but its headwaters are found in the Owyhee Mountains. In fact, native redband trout inhabit even the tiniest of streams in the Owyhee Range, especially in the more remote canyons and ravines of this already-remote area. Each of these trout is a special prize: Their exquisite color and marking make them one the most striking trouts, though a large fish spans but ten inches. Anglers who venture to this remote region should take special care to release these beautiful specimens.

Should you travel to this country—the Owyhee River, the South Fork Owyhee, the Little Owyhee or the tiny streams of the Owyhee Mountains—carry extra everything: tires, fuel, oil, water, food, clothing, emergency equipment and so on. Also, take good maps, such as the BLM sectionals and the USGS topo maps. Throughout this vast expanse, access is primarily by 4X4 and by foot. In some places, private ranch holdings block access. You can try to find a door to knock on, but even doing that is often a difficult task. My preference is to park the truck in some hidden clump of junipers, hike into one of the many canyons and fish up or down the creek well away from the ranchers and their activities.

Sheep Creek Reservoir/Mountain View Reservoir

Located on the Duck Valley Indian Reservation, which straddles the Idaho/Nevada border almost due south of Mountain Home, these two rainbow trout reservoirs offer excellent prospects most years. Sheep Creek, traditionally at least, is the better and more popular of the two. Both are good float-tube waters. Furthermore, as of this writing, the tribal fish and game agency is planning to build a third reservoir that will be managed for trophy trout. Ground breaking was scheduled to occur in 1997, so the late 90s could bring another excellent float-tube water to the reservation.

Tribal permits are required and are available at various locations in Idaho, and from the reservation agent who patrols the reservoirs. Check with Boise and Twin Falls fly shops to find current distributors of the inexpensive permits or call the tribal fish & game office at 702/757-2921.

To reach the reservation, follow State Route 51 south out of Mountain Home and keep going until you reach the reservation boundary just south of Riddle. Mountain View Reservoir will be on your right before you cross into Nevada and Sheep Creek is located a short distance across the border.

Both reservoirs are rich in aquatic trout foods, with scuds being a significant item in the diet of the fast-growing rainbows. Also abundant are damsels, snails, *Callibaetis* mayflies, water beetles, boatmen, backswimmers, Chironomids, dragonflies and leeches. Fishing is best in spring, between late March and June, and again in the fall.

SALMON REGION

Lemhi River

This little-known and underappreciated river has given me some pleasurable days of fishing through the years, despite the fact that most of the river runs through private property in the expansive Lemhi Valley.

The Lemhi is a small river, flowing northwesterly from its sources above Leadore to its confluence with the Salmon River at the town of Salmon. The best fishing occurs in the agricultural lands between Leadore and Baker. I suspect some good fishing can be had in the short reach from Baker to the Salmon River, though I've never gone in search of access here.

Access is indeed the problem on the Lemhi. Three public access sites are located between Tendoy and Leadore, along with a couple of informal access sites along the roads. However, the best fishing is on private property and I've had no problems getting access with a knock on a door or two. Rainbows predominate, but depending on which reach you fish, you may also find cutthroat, cutt-bows, and brook trout. Bull trout survive in places. Hopper season is best (July through September).

Follow Hwy. 28 north from southeast Idaho. You can reach Hwy. 28 via Interstate 15 out of Idaho Falls. From the west, shoot across the desert through Arco until you reach the Hwy. 20/Hwy. 33 intersection, which points you towards Howe. Follow Hwy. 33/22 up to Howe and continue east. Continue past the Mud Lake turnoff (Hwy. 33) and turn northwesterly on Hwy. 28. The Hwy. 28 turnoff (to the north) is just beyond the Clark/Butte County Line, 14 miles past the Mud Lake intersection.

Middle Fork Salmon River

Entirely within the confines of the 2.2-million-acre Frank Church River Of No Return Wilderness Area, the Middle Fork of the Salmon defines the essence of a wild river. Its rugged white water is the stuff of legend and its recovered population of unique westslope cutthroat —protected since 1970 by Idaho's first catch-and-release regulation—attack dry-flies with unabashed enthusiasm.

The Middle Fork makes for a memorable float as it is laden with heavy white water. Splash-and-giggle outfits—kayakers and rafters—far outnumber serious anglers. Hire a guide if you wish to float this river; even experienced white water floaters shouldn't attempt the Middle Fork without first going with someone who knows the river. You'll need a week or so to make the journey.

The only drive-in access to the river leads to Dagger Falls not far from the headwaters. To reach Dagger Falls, follow Hwy. 21 northeast from Lowman or northwest from Stanley to Forest Service Road 198/579, which leads up to Bear Valley Creek. Turn right (north) on FR 568 at Bruce Meadows. Continue north, past Camptender Campground and continue down Dagger Creek until you reach the falls. The boat put-in is just downstream at Boundary Creek.

Numerous wilderness trails reach the river along its 100-plus-mile course. Most require rather lengthy journeys, but many follow productive, cutthroat-laden tributaries. Parts of both Bear Valley Creek and Meadow Creek, which converge to form the Middle Fork's headwaters, offer excellent hike-in fishing. Other good fisheries include Sulphur Creek, Soldier Creek, Pistol Creek, Indian Creek, Marble Creek, Loon Creek, Camas Creek, Big Creek, Rapid River and several others.

The U.S. Forest Service publishes an excellent waterproof map of the Middle Fork as well as a two-map set of the Frank Church River Of No Return Wilderness. Also, you will need a wilderness permit to float the river. For maps and permits, contact the Middle Fork Ranger District at 208-879-4101 or call the Forest Supervisor's office at 208/879-2285. You can obtain a list of Middle Fork guides and outfitters by contacting Idaho Outfitters & Guides Association at 208/342-1438. If you tackle the river on your own, first get a copy of *Handbook to the Middle Fork of the Salmon River*, from Frank Amato Publications of Portland, Oregon (503/653-8108). Many Idaho book stores and outdoor stores carry this title as well.

Upper Salmon River
(Stanley Basin to Corn Creek)

The main Salmon River upstream from the Wild & Scenic wilderness section is best known for its steelhead fishing for A-run fish averaging four to 10 pounds. These steelhead arrive during mid- to late fall, offering fair to good prospects between Corn Creek and the town of Salmon, sometimes higher. The fishing picks up again in early spring (March and April) when the steelhead resume their migration. The spring fishing can be good all the way up to Stanley Basin.

Because water temperatures hover in the 40s during spring, most fishing is done with high-density, sink-tip lines or full-sinking heads. Popular flies include traditional steelhead patterns such as the Purple Peril, Green-Butt Skunk and Golden Demon, but Spey-style flies have increasingly gained a following on the Salmon River.

Access is good along most of the river, as Route 75 and Highway 93, respectively, follow the Salmon from Stanley Basin all the way to North Fork. At North Fork, Forest Service Road 030 follows the river west some 40 miles to Corn Creek, where the road ends and where the Salmon enters the Frank Church Wilderness Area. Private property in the Salmon area limits walk-in access to some excellent water, but anglers can drift the river in any number of places: Launches south of Salmon are located at Shoup Bridge four miles south of town; at Deer Gulch, 3 miles north of Ellis; at Ellis itself; 10 miles north of Challis at Cottonwood. Several ramps are located downstream (north) of Salmon, the best being at Morgan Bar, Tower Rock, Red Rock and North Fork. Below North Fork, you are limited to three take-outs: Deadwater, just west of town, Cache Bar near the mouth of the Middle Fork, and Corn Creek.

Steelhead of 12 to 18 pounds, most of them hatchery fish like this 15-pound specimen, draw fly anglers from all quarters to the Clearwater during fall.

Trout fishing in the Salmon is fair to good for hatchery rainbows and wild cutthroats. The best water for cutthroats is the water least accessible from the road. Midsummer offers hatches of stoneflies and caddis, but high water can make for slow dry-fly action. The best trout fishing occurs from mid-August through October. Grasshoppers abound along the river by late summer and this situation, combined with low flows, creates an ideal opportunity to work out-of-the-way pockets, edges and pools with hopper patterns. Autumn also brings strong hatches of blue-winged olives and mahogany duns on certain parts of the river.

Frank Church River of No Return Wilderness

In addition to its countless fishable streams, this vast wilderness area offers many fishable mountain lakes. To plan an alpine-lake fishing trip in the wilderness, first study the topo maps available from the Forest Service. Then contact IDFG to get current stocking information for particular lakes or lake basins. Depending on elevation and exposure, most lakes become accessible during July and remain accessible until the first autumn snows (typically mid- to late September).

A perusal of the maps will reveal lots of isolated lakes, which often offer total solitude—especially if no trails reach them. The major lake basins and clusters are more popular, but even these areas offer lots of isolation and solitude to go along with good trout fishing and spectacular landscapes. Once you've decided on a destination, purchase the U.S. Geological Survey maps for that area. These large-scale topographical maps are invaluable for cross-country travel in the wilderness. They are available at outdoor stores, book stores, and from the USGS itself, which can be reached at the following address: USGS Map Distribution, Western Branch; Box 25286, Federal Building 41, Denver, CO 80225.

Dozens of small lakes, many quite isolated, dot the mountains between the upper Middle Fork on the west and Rapid River on the east. These include the Vanity Lakes, Soldier Lakes and many others. The beautiful Bighorn Crags, near the lower end of the Middle Fork, hide dozens more pristine lakes, many of which offer excellent fishing in total seclusion. Cutthroat trout abound, along with a few brook trout. In a few lakes, golden trout reward long excursions.

Pahsimeroi River

The Pahsimeroi River is a little-known cutthroat and rainbow stream (along with brook and bull trout) that enters the Salmon River at Ellis after flowing northwesterly out of the northeast slope of the Lost River Range. The Pahsimeroi's best reaches flow almost entirely through private lands in the Pahsimeroi Valley, but many of the residents will grant permission to anglers. Most trout will be less than 12 inches, but 14- to 18-inch cutthroat and rainbows are plentiful enough to provide a surprise now and then.

The diminutive upper river flows through national forest and BLM lands and provides good fishing for small trout in a remote setting. Roads follow the valley on both sides of the river. A somewhat confusing network of primitive roads access the upper river, so be sure to consult a good map (Salmon National Forest). Like many small streams in central Idaho, you can have this water all to yourself most of the time.

Williams Lake offers good float-tube fishing for rainbows that can reach 20 inches.

Williams Lake

Williams Lake is located about 12 miles south of Salmon in the foothills above the Salmon River's west bank. This is excellent float-tube water, especially at the upper end where the creek enters the lake. The lake's rainbows commonly range from 12 to 16 inches with fish to 20 inches available. Typically they are fat, healthy trout. A mid- to late-summer *Callibaetis* hatch provides good dry-fly angling when the wind stays down. Good wet-flies include leeches, scuds, *Callibaetis* nymphs and Carey Specials. The short gravel road leading to the lake crosses the Salmon River at Shoup Bridge off Hwy. 93 south of town. You'll see the signs. A resort and quite a few homes look out over the 230-acre lake, so

the best access is at the top end or from the boat ramp along the north shore. An occasional bull trout is caught in addition to the naturally reproducing rainbows.

Bayhorse Lakes

These two popular and beautiful lakes lay west of the Salmon River, south of Challis. A campground with all the amenities is located at the big lake. Both lakes offer rainbows that can reach surprising size, although they are primarily put-and-take fisheries. Little Bayhorse is the less pressured of the two. Forest Service Road 051 leads up to the lakes from Hwy. 75 about nine miles south of the 75/93 junction near Challis.

Sawtooth Wilderness and the White Cloud Peaks

The eastern edge of the Sawtooth Wilderness is located within the Salmon region. Included are popular lakes like Hell Roaring and Imogene, along with ever-popular Redfish Lake which lies on the wilderness border. These lakes produce good catches and the many smaller lakes located in the higher basins above can provide a combination of good fishing, great scenery, and solitude. U.S. Geological Survey topographical maps are a must for serious wilderness travelers and you can check with the ranger stations in the area for current conditions.

Across the Sawtooth Valley, to the east of the spectacular Sawtooth Mountains, the massive White Cloud Peaks dominate the horizon. A venture into these mountains will be rewarded with excellent alpine-lake fishing at any number of pristine lakes. At 11,830 feet, Castle Peak is the highest of several tremendous mountains. Study a topo map and then call IDFG for current stocking information on particular lakes. Brook trout, cutthroat and golden trout are available.

Find the right lake in the Sawtooths and you may find surprisingly large cutthroat like this one, which came from a small lake at about 10,000 feet in elevation.

JOHN SHEWEY

NORTHERN IDAHO CLEARWATER & PANHANDLE REGIONS

The Clearwater region is named for the Clearwater River, which drains a tremendous chunk of central north-central Idaho. For the dry-fly enthusiast, the cutthroat streams of the Clearwater region have become a Mecca of sorts. The Lochsa River and Kelly Creek are well-known for their exquisite waters and elegant westslope cutthroat. Less known outside the area is the Selway River, a spectacular white water gem whose course is largely enveloped by the Selway-Bitterroot Wilderness. The Selway is one of Idaho's best-kept secrets for it offers an abundance of eager cutthroat in a truly magnificent setting. The many miles of wilderness hiking or floating required to discover its nature assures that this verdant stream will remain a reminder of what so many Rocky Mountain rivers once were.

As exceptional as the cutthroat fishing can be on these special streams, many anglers devote their time to a more addicting pursuit in the region: fly fishing for steelhead on the Clearwater River above Lewiston. Having negotiated a gauntlet of dams on the Columbia and Snake rivers, Clearwater River steelhead arrive between late August and October. Despite their arduous journey (or perhaps because of it), these Clearwater River steelhead are big and strong and full of fight. Twelve- to 18-pound fish are typical.

Native cutthroat abound in the streams of central and northern Idaho. This specimen came from a tributary to the Selway.

The Lochsa ranks as one of the most beautiful
trout streams anywhere.

The Clearwater is a very accessible river, as is the popular Lochsa, one of its upstream tributaries. These streams contrast vividly with the likes of Kelly Creek and the Selway, which remain isolated by long, rough roads or by no roads at all.

Anglers in the Clearwater region face but one real problem: Everything good happens about the same time. No sooner have the cutthroat streams dropped to their imminently fishable August/September levels, than the steelhead begin to appear in the Clearwater. This can be a tough place to make choices, but those are the kind of choices we like.

Just to the north, Idaho's Panhandle Region offers another set of productive fisheries for the native westslope cutthroat. The St. Joe River is the most popular of these, in fact it is the most popular trout stream in northern Idaho; its cutthroat fishery offers a study in contrasts to the North Fork Coeur d'Alene watershed to the north. The North Fork offers decent fishing in a lovely setting, but its watershed has suffered heavy losses at the hands of man. Where the St. Joe features trout-filled pools stacked together in many places, the North Fork offers long, barren expanses of shallow riffle water between its remnant pools. Hence the population of trout per river mile is far less in the North Fork than in the St. Joe.

Still, the same native cutthroat cling to existence in the North Fork Coeur d'Alene and its tributaries, even thriving in some of the deeper pools of the catch-and-release section. These beautiful westslope cutthroat evolved here and have existed in these drainages since the last ice-age receded. They are perfectly adapted to the mountain-stream habitat, and given half a chance by wise land-use practices and insightful resource management, these cutthroat will continue to thrive in northern Idaho.

The St. Joe and North Fork Coeur d'Alene offer the top prospects for these unique and striking cutthroat, but many smaller streams also provide good summer and autumn angling. Forest Service travel maps will help you locate small forested streams that you can have to yourself.

Stillwater opportunities in the panhandle range from expansive Priest Lake to the diminutive hike-in lakes of the Selkirk Mountains. The more adventuresome fly angler might want to sample the region's tremendous warm-water opportunities: Sprawling Coeur d'Alene Lake offers a chance at large northern pike during late spring and early summer. Largemouth bass are abundant here, too, although the Chain Lakes, which feed the southeast arm of Coeur d'Alene Lake, are the better choice for bass, crappie and sunfish enthusiasts.

The town of Coeur d'Alene is a tourist destination with all the trappings, including a fly shop and a popular golf course featuring a floating green. Sandpoint, likewise, is a tourist draw on a smaller scale. Both towns feature attractive little downtown areas. Despite the growing population in the Idaho Panhandle, the St. Joe River seems to attract as many or more anglers from Washington and Montana than from Idaho—or at least that has been my observation.

Lochsa River

One the state's most scenic and accessible rivers, the beautiful Lochsa River flows southwest out of the Bitterroot Mountains on the Montana border, joining the Selway more than 60 miles downstream. Virtually all of the river is paralleled by Hwy. 12, so anglers have no problem accessing the river and its colorful native cutthroat.

The upper river, from Wilderness Gateway Campground upstream, is catch-and-release water. The remaining stretch downstream from Wilderness Gateway to the confluence with the Selway is managed as wild trout water (artificials only, two-trout limit with none under 14 inches). All tributaries are closed until July 1 to protect spawning cutthroat and all have a two-fish limit during the open season (July 1 to Nov. 30).

Flowing through a mountain canyon cloaked in lush coniferous forest, the Lochsa ranks among the most beautiful of trout streams. The river is characterized by extensive cobblestone flats and riffles interrupted by deeper pools and boulder-strewn runs. After run-off, the water typically runs exquisitely clear and cold. Trout congregate in the deeper pools and runs and in the extensive pocket water. The wide, shallow cobblestone glides hold trout as well, but not in great numbers. In places, rip-rap highway embankments create deep, swirling pockets where huge boulders provide perfect hiding places for large trout.

Many of the Lochsa's cutthroat barely stretch 10 inches, but 12- to 14-inch trout are common and an occasional 18-inch trout will reward those willing to fish the hard-to-reach spots. These beautiful natives

In the Salish tongue, Lochsa means rough water.

Lochsa cutthroat can reach impressive size, but hooking these large specimens often requires that you seek out-of-the-way pools and make careful presentations.

exhibit a range of markings, with some of the larger specimens elegantly adorned with reddish gill covers and broad blaze-orange bellies.

Frequently these cutthroat will pounce on basic attractor-style dry-flies like Royal Wulffs, Elk Hair Caddis, Humpies and Renegades. Late afternoon and evening caddis hatches can trigger localized, selective feeding and many of the large trout fall to anglers who recognize those trout that are feeding on a specific insect.

Many anglers, passing between points west and the waters of Montana, fish the Lochsa on their way through, the river's promising beauty is simply too much to ignore. Many such anglers fish only the easy-access and easy-to-wade places near the highway; catch-and-release regulations assure that these places hold trout. Serious Lochsa regulars pursue a different strategy: They seek the hard-to-fish areas, including pools, runs and pockets away from the road as well as the rip-rap embankments that are too steep and intimidating for most folks; they look for pools where a long cast from a high boulder offers the only chance, or where a deep wade offers positioning for waters not fishable from the highway side.

First-time Lochsa anglers may want to visit the river during August or September, when low summer flows reveal the streambed's nature. Early season anglers must contend with the high flows of the run-off period, which can last well into July. However, July holds the promise of fishing dry stonefly patterns during the golden stonefly hatch.

Opinions will vary on productive Lochsa River fly patterns, but the following list will serve you well: Elk Hair Caddis, size 12-16; Blue-winged Olive Compara-dun or Sparkle Dun, size 16-20; Renegade, size 12-18; Humpy and Royal Wulff, size 12-16; hopper patterns, size 8-10; Golden Stones (I use Maxwell's Jughead), size 6-10; Yellow Sally (yellow Elk Hair Caddis or Lawson Yellow Sallys), size 12-14; Black Flying Ant, size 12-14; Gulper Special, Olive and Cream, size 12-16; X-Caddis, size 14-16. Hare's Ear Nymph, Pheasant Tail, dark stonefly nymph, Peeking Caddis and other such standbys will take care of any sub-surface needs; soft-hackle wet-flies can be deadly at times.

Campsites are plentiful along the Lochsa. Wilderness Gateway Campground at the lower end of the catch-and-release section boasts 88 camp units. Moving upriver, you will find Jerry Johnson Campground (15 sites), Wendover Campground (28 sites), Whitehouse Campground (14 sites), Powell Campground (37 sites) and, at the Lochsa's headwaters formed by the confluence of Crooked Fork and White Sand creeks, White Sand Campground (5 sites). Unimproved sites are available as well—just scout out the nearest spur road leading off the highway.

For much of its length, the Lochsa's south bank parallels the northern boundary of the 1,337,910-acre Selway-Bitterroot Wilderness. Inside this expansive wilderness, anglers can explore many high lakes and countless small cutthroat streams. Major trail-heads leave the Lochsa at Wilderness Gateway, Eagle Mountain Pack Bridge, Mocus Point Pack Bridge and Jerry Johnson Pack Bridge. Other access sites can be found south of the Lochsa's headwater area. Wilderness travelers should obtain maps from the Forest Service and U.S. Geological Survey.

Kelly Creek

Kelly Creek is one of Idaho's most famous streams owing to its exceptional westslope cutthroat fishery—a fishery that had been severely damaged by overharvest of fish and by land-use practices during the middle of this century.

During the early 1970s, however, Kelly Creek became one of Idaho's first catch-and-release streams. The recovery of the cutthroat population has since been well documented and today this picturesque mountain stream offers a fly angling experience that is hard to equal anywhere in the West, except for perhaps on the similar North Fork Clearwater or Selway rivers.

Isolated by its remoteness, Kelly Creek flows cold and clean from the Bitterroot Range. Its boulder and cobble-strewn path carves out a forested canyon as the creek glides toward its confluence with the North Fork of the Clearwater. Between July and September—the primary fishing season on Kelly Creek—the water flows remarkably and deceptively clear. Sneak up to a vantage point overlooking a glassy pool and you will see cutthroat so plainly that you can count their spots.

Cast a dry-fly to these colorful natives and you can watch, holding your breath, as a ghostly figure glides unhurriedly to the surface to inhale the offering.

Like westslope cutts in other regional drainages, Kelly Creek trout are migratory. They ascend the stream and its tributaries during the late spring spawning season and then dwell in the creek until early autumn. Then they work their way back down to the over-wintering pools of the North Fork Clearwater.

Kelly Creek's run-off subsides by early July in most years and the low water levels of August and September provide ideal dry-fly conditions. A host of basic dry-fly attractors will generally suffice. Among the multitude of productive choices are the following: hoppers, Humpy, Renegade, Parachute Adams, Elk Hair Caddis, Madam-X and Gulper Special.

In the more heavily fished sections along the road, the larger cutthroat (14- to 20-inch specimens) tend to get educated quickly each season—not so dramatically as on the Lochsa and St. Joe, but educated nonetheless.

If you get refusals from these larger fish, try switching to smaller, more realistic patterns. Among my favorites are a size 14-16 X-Caddis, size 14 Black Ant, size 18 Griffith's Gnat, size 16-18 Olive Sparkle Dun and size 18 olive Gulper Special. A soft-hackle wet-fly, fished just a few inches below the surface, can be deadly.

The lower half of Kelly Creek's 20-plus-mile course is followed by Forest Service Road 255, which provides easy access to many exquisite trout-filled pools and runs. If you prefer water more private, lace up the boots and hike the upper 12 miles of the creek. The scenery alone is worth the effort, and the fishing can be fast and furious.

Kelly Creek.

A good trail follows the north bank above Kelly Creek Ranger Station. A 4-1/2-mile trek will take you to the mouth of Cayuse Creek, one of the major tributaries. Cayuse offers the same kind of fishing for those willing to walk. Kelly Creek gathers its headwaters another six to seven miles upstream, above Hanson Meadows: The South Fork, Middle Fork and North Fork drain the crest and west slope of the Bitterroots.

Cayuse Creek is accessible by road about five miles above its confluence with Kelly Creek. When you reach the junction of FR 255 and 581 (where the roadless section of Kelly Creek begins), turn south on 581 (Tobaggan Ridge Road) and wind up the hill for some nine miles until you cross Cayuse Creek. You can hike up or down from there.

Even the roaded section of Kelly Creek is quite remote, requiring a 40-mile drive over gravel roads from Superior, Montana or a 50-mile journey on gravel from Pierce, Idaho. Pierce is located east of Orofino and you can get there via Route 11, which leaves Hwy. 12 a few miles southeast of Orofino, or via Grangemont Road, which heads easterly out of Orofino and connects with Route 11 just north of Pierce.

Just south of Pierce, head easterly on FR 250 until you reach the North Fork Clearwater River. Cross the river and turn right (east), following FR 250 up to Kelly Forks Ranger Station. The road continues along Kelly Creek for 11 miles before turning north to Ruby Creek Campground.

From Superior, Montana, follow Trout Creek Road (FR 250) over Hoodoo Pass and then down past Cedars Campground on the North Fork Clearwater. Follow the river on FR 250 until you reach the intersection with FR 255. FR 255 heads south to Kelly Creek Ranger Station; FR 250 crosses the North Fork and then follows the river down to Kelly Forks Ranger Station. FR 255 is faster, but 250 takes you along some prime trout water on the North Fork.

Campgrounds are located at Kelly Forks (14 sites) and upstream at Ruby Creek (near Kelly Creek Ranger Station). Rough camping sites are abundant in the area.

A third route to Kelly Creek leaves Hwy. 12 at Powell on the Lochsa River and follows Parachute Hill Road (FR569) up to Papoose Saddle, then FR 500 west to Tobaggan Ridge Road (FR 581), which eventually crosses Cayuse Creek and drops down to Kelly Creek. This is the roughest going of the three routes and you should check road conditions ahead of time by calling the Clearwater National Forest.

North Fork Clearwater

Home to spectacular summer steelhead before Dworshak Dam doomed the once-substantial run, the North Fork Clearwater is now a remote and productive cutthroat/rainbow fishery with ten- to 18-inch trout being typical.

This artificials-only river is a mix of elegant glassy pools, gliding runs and wide riffles, all of it swirling through a forested canyon littered with boulders, cobble and gravel.

Summer fishing is good, but by September and October, cutthroat from upriver tributaries (like Kelly Creek) have migrated back down to their wintering pools on the North Fork. At this time of year (mid-September through October) fly anglers can have vast reaches of the North Fork all to themselves with the promise of good numbers of 12- to 20-inch cutthroat waiting to reward their efforts.

A sporadic hatch of October caddis (giant orange sedge) graces some sections of the river on warm autumn evenings. Smaller caddis abound and some dense hatches occur summer and early fall. Blue-winged olive mayflies emerge on cloudy September days. Golden stoneflies appear in July, as do little yellow stones (yellow Sallies). Hopper patterns can be very productive during August and September.

Forest Service roads parallel the entire North Fork, making for easy access. From Pierce, Idaho, follow FR 250 northeasterly to the river (on the way to Kelly Creek) and fish either direction. The section downstream from the bridge on FR 250 is followed by FR 247 all the way to the Dworshak Reservoir backwaters. Near Canyon Ranger Station, a few miles above the reservoir, FR 247 crosses the river and heads south back to Pierce. Meanwhile, the beautiful upper reaches of the North Fork are accessed via FR 250. Seven campgrounds line the river.

Selway River

The Selway River rivals the Lochsa in sheer beauty and for much of its length surpasses its northerly neighbor in the quality of its cutthroat fishery—namely because the Selway is a wilderness river where hike-in (and a few float-in) anglers never encounter the crowds that sometimes converge on the Lochsa.

Named for a Montana sheepman Thomas Selway, the Selway River runs some 75 miles from it headwaters in the Bitterroot Mountains to its confluence with the Lochsa. The lower 19 miles are accessible by road; on the upper river, about 15 miles of water are accessible by road in the Magruder Corridor area between Elk City, Idaho and Conner, Montana. Everything in between is hike-in or float-in only as the river plummets through the Selway-Bitterroot Wilderness Area.

Floating the Selway is a coveted privilege enjoyed by only a few dozen parties each year, most of these being white-water enthusiasts. A limited number of permits are available each season and only one launch per day is allowed from the Paradise Launch just outside the southern boundary of the wilderness northeast of Elk City. The wilderness reach of the river, which draws white-water enthusiasts and anglers alike, flows precipitously through a boulder-strewn canyon where class III and IV rapids await. Late summer and early fall are the best times for fly anglers: By August, the water is low and clear; easy to fish and fairly easy to wade.

Beautiful native cutthroat up to 14 inches are common; 14- to 18-inch trout are fairly common as well. Bull trout inhabit the deeper runs and pools. By late summer, the Selway offers an abundance of classic dry-fly pocket water divided at intervals by glassy pools and runs. The fishing is uncomplicated and rewarding. An Elk Hair Caddis, Jug Head, Parachute Adams or just about any other favorite dry fly will do the trick.

To reach the Selway River where it exits the wilderness (Selway Falls), follow Hwy. 12 from Kooskia east to Lowell, then turn south along the Selway River up to Selway Falls and Race Creek Campground. The trailhead begins here and leads eastward into the wilderness. As you might expect, the farther you walk, the better the fishing.

To reach Magruder Corridor and Paradise (the upstream entrance to the wilderness), follow Hwy. 95 to Grangeville and then turn east on Route 13 and travel easterly some eight miles to the Route 14 turnoff. Route 14 takes you east to Elk City and from there follow the Magruder Corridor Road (FR 468) southeast, east and then north to the river at Magruder Crossing. FR 6223 turns north after you cross the bridge and follows the river up to Paradise.

If you are coming from southeast Idaho, head toward Darby and Hamilton, Montana via Hwy. 93 through Salmon or via I-15. South of Darby, watch for Forest Service Road 473 at Conner, Montana and follow this road over Nez Perce Pass and down to the Selway.

From either direction, you are looking at a long, rough drive where a four-wheel-drive vehicle with good clearance is optimum. The river along the road between Magruder Crossing and Paradise offers good fishing. For information on float permits (and for other wilderness information) contact the Bitterroot National Forest in Darby at (406) 821-3269.

Clearwater River

Idaho's Clearwater River is home to a truly remarkable race of summer steelhead. These fish, called the "B-runs," are large steelhead, typically topping the scales at 12 to 18 pounds. Their unlikely journey to and from the Pacific takes them through a gauntlet of dams on the Columbia and then through four more dams on the Snake River. The only thing more amazing than the fact that Clearwater River smolt make it to the Pacific is the additional fact that any adults at all survive the return journey. Indeed these are a remarkable steelhead, despite the fact that the construction of Dwarshak Dam essentially destroyed what was once the greatest steelhead run in the West.

The Clearwater River is famed for its fly-angling opportunity. The best fishing occurs from mid-September on because Dworshak Dam is typically corked about that time, dropping the river to good fishable levels. Late August through mid-September, before the water drops, can offer good fishing as well. In addition to some early B-run steelhead,

smaller A-run fish destined for the Salmon and Snake rivers often hold over in the lower Clearwater during August and September. These fish average four to ten pounds.

The Clearwater enters the Snake at the town of Lewiston and the steelhead fly angling literally begins at Lewiston. A broad, flat run at the Potlatch Mill marks the first popular fly-angling pool, although this water leaves a lot to be desired if you like traditional steelhead habitat. In fact, the lower few miles of the river are characterized by broad, low-gradient steelhead pools that in some cases take hours to fish from top to bottom. These are productive waters, however, so they are heavily fished.

I prefer the water above the Hwy. 95 bridge some six miles above Lewiston. Here the river's gradient steepens a bit, creating a variety of classic-type runs and pools. Difficult wading is the rule when the flows are up during August and early September, but if you pick your spots and are a practiced caster, you will find the Clearwater comparatively uncrowded. The first day the water drops coincides with a rush of local fly anglers and from then through October and even early November you can expect plenty of company on the river. Increasingly, fly anglers are working the river well into winter.

Fly patterns vary from angler to angler, but a variety of classic hairwing steelhead flies, Spey-style flies and skating flies are popular. The Clearwater is indeed a good dry-fly river when water temperatures remain in the 50s or a little higher. Part of its allure is an abundance of glass-smooth, shallow "skater water."

The Clearwater River is renowned for its run of B-strain steelhead.

The author with a Clearwater River wild steelhead.

Most of the time a floating line and a wet-fly, fished on a down-and-across swing will do the job. As autumn wears on and water temperatures plummet, you may want to switch to a sink-tip or sinking line so you can swing the fly deep and slow. During periods of bright, midday sunlight, a sink-tip will help keep the fly just below the glare layer, allowing fish a better chance to see your offering.

Highway 12 runs along the Clearwater River all the way to the forks, so access is easy. You will find private property in places, but a knock on the land owner's door can solve that problem.

Little North Fork Clearwater

A remote hike-in mountain stream harboring native cutthroat, bull trout, whitefish and residualized steelhead, the latter a remnant of what was once one of the world's great steelhead runs—a run that was completely obliterated by the construction of Dworshak Dam.

Cuts average eight to 12 inches but reach 18 inches in this beautiful and lightly fished stream. Consult the Idaho Panhandle National Forest Travel Map for Avery of the St. Joe Ranger District.

Main Salmon River (Corn Creek to mouth)

The remarkable Salmon River flows free for more than 400 miles on a journey that takes it through one of America's most awesome wilderness expanses. Along the way, this fabled river carves out a massive canyon whose depth is exceeded in North America only by Hells Canyon on the Snake River. Fittingly, the Salmon eventually yields its waters to Hells Canyon.

The Salmon's wilderness reach—some 100 miles of untamed rapids interrupted in turn by placid pools and clean sand beaches—attracts white-water enthusiasts from all quarters. Legendary Class III and IV rapids include places such as Big Mallard, Split Rock and Chittam. Native cutthroat, wild rainbows, whitefish and bull trout inhabit the main Salmon, but in the wilderness section at least, white water thrills and backcountry vacations are the primary draw. Should you decide to make the trip, a guided venture is the prudent choice for your first time at least. Outfitters can be contacted through the Idaho Guides & Outfitters Association.

The lower end of the river carves yet another impressive canyon through isolated sage and cheatgrass steppe before finally yielding to the massive Snake River below. In this reach, steelhead anglers can intercept the fish as they enter the river in prime condition between late August and late October. late September and October are best. Jet-boaters can run up from below or drifters can make multi-day floats from Pine Bar, west of Grangeville. Shorter floats are possible by launching at points upstream from Pine Bar. A few primitive roads approach the canyon off Divide Creek Road to the south and near Keuterville on the north. The lower canyon is good chukar country as well, and several Salmon River outfitters and guides offer combination steelhead/chukar trips.

St. Joe River

The exquisite St. Joe River stands as the premier trout stream in the Idaho Panhandle, its notoriety having reached regional and even national status over the past decade. This beautiful mountain stream emanates from the Bitterroot Range, which forms the Montana/Idaho border along much of the panhandle's eastern edge.

According to IDFG, more than 30 percent of the westslope cutthroat in the catch-and-release section of the St. Joe are more than a foot in length. Snorkeling studies done in the early 90s indicated that the St. Joe supports a higher density of cutthroat than any of the other north Idaho cutthroat streams—including the Lochsa, North Fork of the Clearwater and Coeur d'Alene rivers and even higher than famed Kelly Creek. The snorkeling studies, conducted by Joel Hunt and summarized by Regional biologist Ned Horner in a 1993 *Idaho Wildlife* article, found that fish numbers ranged from 344 to 732 cutthroat per mile in the St. Joe's catch-and-release sections and from 98 to 162 fish per mile in the limited-harvest sections.

The St. Joe is classic westslope cutthroat water, with shallow cobblestone flats interrupted at every bend and turn by pocket water, smooth glides and bubbleshot pools, whose deep, swirling waters generally hold schools of cutthroat from 10 to 18 inches. This is dry-fly water, where attractor patterns do most of the work. Still, the extensive pressure from fly anglers has served to educate many of the larger fish to the point that long before mid-season they become highly suspicious of high-floating attractors. (Regional Biologist Ned Horner characterizes the pressure on the St. Joe as "heavy," saying the river "has been discovered.")

Anglers who recognize this fact fool the big fish on small, sparse flies, including Griffith's Gnats, ant patterns, small parachute flies, floating nymphs and various other spring-creek-type dressings. Caddis hatches can be heavy at times, especially during summer evenings. The St. Joe supports a good population of large stoneflies, whose emergence triggers great dry-fly action when it coincides with fishable early-season water levels.

Late summer brings small yellow stoneflies as well as terrestrials and localized mayfly hatches. An effective method for fishing the St. Joe is to cover productive water with an attractor pattern such as a Royal Wulff, Humpy, St. Joe Special, Renegade or hopper and keep a sharp eye out for visible refusals—trout that glide up as if to take the fly, but turn away short of rising. When this happens, rest the trout while switching to a small, inoffensive pattern and try again.

St. Joe cutthroat.

Most fly anglers concentrate on the 15-mile reach from Spruce Tree Campground (upstream from the ranger station at Red Ives) down to Gold Creek Road, which is the access road that comes over the mountains from St. Regis, Montana. This is all catch-and-release water, as is the entire river and its tributaries all the way down to Prospector Creek, another 15-odd-mile stretch. Below Gold Creek, the river gains momentum and size as it roars through several major rapids popular with whitewater enthusiasts. Less utilized by fly anglers, the catch-and-release waters below Gold Creek offer fishing every bit as productive, especially for those willing to wade aggressively and fish pockets and pools not reached by most anglers.

Likewise, the roadless area above Spruce Tree Campground is less pressured than the rest of the river and the farther you walk upstream, the fewer people you will find.

From Prospector Creek all the way down to the town of St. Maries, current regulations allow anglers to keep one cutthroat 14 inches or over. This stretch is planted with legal-sized rainbow trout as well. Fishing improves as you head upriver from St. Maries, leaving behind the slow water that these cutthroat abandon during the warm summer months. From its confluence with the North Fork of the St. Joe near Avery, the river offers excellent summer fishing all the way through the white water section, past Prospector and Gold creeks and all the way into its headwaters.

Several campgrounds and numerous unimproved campsites line the river from Avery to Spruce Tree Campground. The route from St. Regis, Montana follows Little Joe Road out of the west end of town, over I-90, and into the mountains. A mile and a half out of St. Regis the pavement ends and you will follow 15 miles of good gravel road to reach the summit (and the state line). Gold Creek Road, down the Idaho side, is paved but narrow and winding for 12 miles down to the St. Joe.

A second route leaves I-90 at the quaint historic mining town of Wallace, Idaho (east of Coeur d'Alene), climbs over Moon Pass and leads down the North Fork St. Joe to reach the mainstem at Avery. Bullion Creek Road, just east of the state line also accesses the river. The Little Joe Road from St. Regis was a better route than either of these two others last time I was there. From the west, follow I-90 out of Coeur d'Alene to Highway 3, which runs through the Chain Lakes along the lower Coeur d'Alene River (these contain bass, pike, and panfish). When you reach the town of St. Maries, head east along the St. Joe River Road, following the river on pavement for more than 100 miles all the way to Red Ives.

The St. Joe Ranger District Map shows the entire area in up-to-date status. These are available free of charge from any of the area Forest Service offices and from the Coeur d'Alene Visitor's Center.

Boyd Matson of Spokane fishes the St. Joe
during late summer.

North Fork Coeur d'Alene River

As a scenic mountain stream that supports wild cutthroat trout, the North Fork of the Coeur d'Alene River is similar in many regards to the St. Joe River, its famous neighbor to the southeast. The St. Joe supports a significantly more dense population of trout, but also attracts more angling pressure, leaving the North Fork mostly to local fly anglers who ply its catch-and-release sections for cutthroat that occasionally reach 20 inches.

After spring run-off, the North Fork in its upper reaches is a small stream where long, shallow riffles with scant trout habitat are interrupted by deeper runs, pools and pockets whose green depths hold cutthroat of surprising length. Many of these beautiful natives stretch 10 to 12 inches, but a hard day's fishing is often rewarded with a 16- to 18-inch cutthroat, maybe two or three such fish.

These westslope cuts of the Coeur d'Alene grow faster than those in the St. Joe, but their numbers are fewer owing to the devastating watershed damage of decades past—damage from logging, mining and road-building activities. Reparations are under way, however, as Forest Service and fish and game officials work to restore the watershed. Meanwhile, fishing steadily improves.

Fly anglers concentrate their efforts in the catch-and-release sections above Yellowdog Creek and on the similar Little North Fork. All tributaries to these sections are catch-and-release as well, and the tributary streams can offer excellent pocket water fishing for those willing to do some walking.

This is classic dry-fly water, offering everything from mysterious, deep pools where the river collides with rock escarpments to gliding runs studded with polished rocks. Any water with a little depth and a little cover is likely to hold fish and the only reaches I habitually ignore are the long, shallow cobblestone flats where insufficient depth means lack of cover and lack of trout.

Furthermore, anglers willing to seek out the pools and runs furthest from the road will often find the best fishing, although even the stretches abutting the road can provide excellent fishing on weekdays when the river sees little pressure.

One of the great attractions of the upper North Fork is the 15-mile-long Coeur d'Alene National Recreation Trail that provides the only easy access for substantial stretches of river above Tepee Creek. Although reduced in size above Tepee Creek, the North Fork nonetheless offers an abundance of nice pocket water along with beautiful pools and glides—all amidst the forest scenery dominated by Cathedral Peak, Cathedral Rocks and Steamboat Rock.

Fly patterns are basic. Attractor dry-flies are the rule although evening caddis hatches make small Elk Hair Caddis patterns especially effective. Blue-winged olives make regular though localized appearances during cool weather. Number 18 and 20 imitations will fool those cutts who prove too suspicious of attractor patterns. Early season stonefly activity can provide great action when water levels cooperate. My typical pattern during the summer and early fall is to fish a small Jug Head or hopper (size 10) and switch to a size 14 or 16 Elk Hair Caddis, Renegade or Gulper Special if I get a visible refusal. (These cutts often glide casually up to examine a large attractor fly only to turn away in refusal, the whole thing being visible to the angler).

The catch-and-release waters, including Yellowdog Creek and all tributaries above Yellowdog Creek and also the Little North Fork above Laverne Creek, open July 1 and close Nov. 30. Snowmelt can keep the river high through early July, depending upon the snowpack during a particular year. For up-to-date information, call Joe Roope's Castaway Fly Shop at 208-765-3133.

To reach the North Fork, drive east on Interstate 90 out of Coeur d'Alene to the town of Kingston. Exit the freeway and head north on the road (FR9) that follows the river. Yellowdog Creek, the lower boundary for the catch-and-release section, is nearly 40 miles upriver from Kingston and the pavement extends another 10 miles beyond that up to Tepee Creek. The trailhead for the Coeur d'Alene Rec. trail is located at Tepee Creek. Several fee campgrounds lie along the river and you will find numerous unimproved campsites as well.

For access to the uppermost reaches of the North Fork (above the

Most cutthroat in the North Fork Coeur d'Alene reside in the river's deeper pools and runs.

north end of the trail), consult the Fernan Ranger District Map (Idaho Panhandle National Forests). For the rest of the river, obtain the Wallace Ranger District Map (Forest Supervisor, 3815 Schreiber Way, Coeur d'Alene, Idaho 83814; 208/752-1221).

Spokane River

This short and marginally productive stretch of the Spokane River runs from the outflow of Post Falls Dam two miles down to the state line, where it is crossed by I-90. Best fished by drifting, boaters can put-in at Corbin Park and take-out a few miles below in Washington at Harvard Road (take the Liberty Lake Exit off I-90 and turn north to reach the river). Take Exit 2 off I-90 (west of Post Falls) and turn south off the offramp. At the second of two stoplights, turn left on Railroad Avenue and drive about a half mile east to the Corbin Park signs. Turn right to reach the park, where any boat you can carry across the gravel beach will do the job. This stretch, which is capable of growing trout quickly, is closed between the end of February and Memorial Day weekend, but is open the balance of the year. As with any tailwater, check the outflows before you launch.

This North Fork Coeur d'Alene cutthroat took a small stonefly dry.

Moyie River

The Moyie River, a tributary to the Kootenai, flows south from Canada and into the Idaho Panhandle. Its upper reaches in Idaho are put-and-take waters planted with rainbows, but the lower river offers several miles of decent two-fish limit, wild trout water near Meadow Creek Campground. Native westslope cutthroat, wild rainbows, rainbow-cutthroat hybrids and an occasional brook trout inhabit this stretch.

Best access is from the campground, which is reached via Meadow Creek Road. Drive north on Highway 95 out of Bonner's Ferry for about three miles to Highway 2. Turn right and drive about two miles until you see the Meadow Creek Road sign on your left. Turn north and drive 10 miles to the campground. Access is difficult along the best section of river, which extends for about three or four miles below Meadow Creek. A rough road parallels the river from well above on its west bank, leading from Meadow Creek Road due south to Highway 2 near the town of Moyie Springs. I recommend shying away from this road if you're not big on steep bushwhacking excursions. Consult the Bonner's Ferry Ranger District Map.

Above Meadow Creek the river is stocked for put-and-take and the gradient lessens, so fly anglers will want to concentrate on the more-difficult-to-access reach below the campground. Caddis are the dominant insects, but the river does offer a decent early summer hatch of giant stoneflies. High water generally lasts through mid- to late June.

Priest Lake/Upper Priest Lake

At 23,360 acres, Priest Lake occupies a large glacial basin west of the Selkirk Mountains northwest of the town of Sandpoint. This beautiful natural lake offers catch-and-release fishing for cutthroat that commonly range from 12 to 15 inches and max out at about 20 inches. Much of the shoreline is private property and inaccessible, but some 15 boat launches surround the lake, many of them private launches that charge a nominal fee. Priest Lake State Park offers some shoreline access and the Lakeshore Trail on the northwest shore accesses about six miles of public shoreline (U.S. Forest Service). Still, a boat offers a distinct advantage on this large lake.

Anglers can start from any of the launches and then concentrate their efforts in the coves, bays and along points and shoal areas. *Callibaetis*, caddis and midge hatches offer surface action while a selection of basic stillwater wet-flies and streamers will produce at other times.

Upper Priest Lake is an exquisite 1,400-acre gem with no road access. To reach Upper Priest, which also offers westslope cutthroat, anglers can hike a two-mile trail (Navigation Trail) from Beaver Creek Campground on the lake's northwest corner. Hike another two miles to fish the upper end of Upper Priest Lake. The other option is to row up the "thorofare" connecting the two lakes, a distance of about two miles (the Thorofare is closed to fishing). When you turn into the Beaver Creek Campground area, look for the sign pointing to "Portage Trail Parking." The canoe route from here spans about 1 3/4 miles.

To reach Priest Lake, follow Highway 2 west out of Sandpoint to the town of Priest River. Then turn north on Route 57, which reaches the southern end of the lake and then swings around to the northwest and roughly parallels about half of the west shoreline. To access the east shoreline, turn right on Coolin Junction (milepost 22) before you reach the lake. This road is paved to within a few miles of Lionshead Campground on the upper end of the lake.

Priest Lake and Upper Priest Lake harbor native populations of bull trout and mountain whitefish in addition to the native cutthroat. Introduced lake trout (mackinaw) reproduce naturally in the lakes and reach 30 pounds or more. A slot limit on Mackinaw protects spawning-age fish. Upper Priest Lake is a catch-and-release fishery for all species and all tributaries to Upper Priest Lake are closed to fishing, including the Upper Priest River and its tributaries. These latter waters are the last strongholds in the entire Priest Lake Drainage for Bull trout and westslope cutthroat and are closed to all fishing to provide haven for these species.

Tributaries to Priest Lake are open only during the months of July and August to fly and artificial lure anglers. The Priest Lake Ranger District Map details the area. Contact the district office at the town of Priest Lake or the main office in Coeur d'Alene.

The Priest River below Priest Lake Outlet Dam is primarily a white-fish fishery and is open year-round. Cutthroat spawn in the river during spring, but perhaps these fish should be left alone at that time of year. Access is limited due to extensive private land. The Lower West Branch of the Priest River is a small stream featuring beaver ponds and small brook trout and small cutthroat. Pressure is light once you get away from the roads, but trout are small. See the Priest Lake Ranger District Map for directions.

St. Maries River

A fair fishery for native cutthroat and stocked rainbow along with some brook trout. Best section is Below Clarkia in Cedar Canyon, a relatively short stretch. Private land between Mashburn and Clarkia limits access to some extent. Below Mashburn, the river gets too warm for trout—which is unfortunate because a reach of several miles here is roadless.

To reach the St. Maries, follow Highway 3 south from the town of St. Maries down to the bridge at Mashburn. From here you can proceed south about two miles and follow Hwy. 3 as it swings east to Santa and then southeast to Clarkia. Be sure to seek permission to cross private land.

Pack River

The small rainbows, cutthroat and bull trout in the Pack River should be left undisturbed—these are juvenile fish that will move down to join their parents in Lake Pend Oreille. Ned Horner, the district biologist for the Panhandle Region, says the only reason the Pack River "is not closed to fishing is because of public pressure." Fly anglers should find concern here because the Pack River is the most significant natural hatchery for the native trout and char of Lake Pend Orielle. Perhaps a few letters to the IDFG in support of a complete closure would lend some support to affording complete protection to these juvenile fish.

For boat anglers, the Spokane River below Post Falls offers close-to-town trout fishing.

Selected Fly Patterns for Idaho Waters

Idaho Lake/Reservoir Flies

Southern Idaho, especially southwestern Idaho, is the birthplace of a number of popular lake/reservoir trout flies developed by the area's legion of stillwater enthusiasts. In the Western United States, anglers from southern Idaho were among the first to embrace the "belly boat" or float tube as an efficient means of fishing the region's productive reservoirs. The flies shown here, many of them classics in the world of stillwater fly angling, were crafted by Dave Tucker after I asked him to reproduce a set of the flies developed by southern Idaho's reservoir experts of the past few decades. Marv Taylor's first book, *Float Tubes, Fly Rods & Other Essays*, gives the complete history of most of these patterns.

Sheep Creek Special (Biggs' Fly)

Hook: 2XL, size 6-14
Body: 4-5 wraps of brown hackle at rear, then olive chenille
Wing: Small bunch of mallard flank fibers extending to hackle at rear
Originator: George Biggs

Stayner Ducktail

Hook: 3XL, size 2-14
Tail: Burnt orange or hot orange hackle fibers
Rib: Gold oval tinsel
Body: Olive chenille
Throat: Burnt orange or hot orange hackle fibers
Wing: Mallard flank feather extending just past tail
Originator: Ruel Stayner

Blonde Stayner

Same as above, but substitute variegated light olive/yellow chenille for the body and lemon wood duck or mallard dyed wood duck for the wing.
Notes: Designed by Marv Taylor to imitate perch minnows in Magic Reservoir.

Tex's Favorite

Hook: 2XL, size 8-12
Tail: Brown hackle fibers
Body: Olive chenille
Hackle: Brown saddle, tied wet-fly style
Notes: Originated by Ken Magee and named for Wayne "Tex" Meeks because of Tex's fondness for the pattern.

Mick's Stick Fly

Hook: 1X or 2XL, size 10-16
Rib: Fine flat or fine oval silver tinsel
Body: Fine grayish-brown wool yarn
Note: Originated by Mick Miller of Nampa, this Chironomid pattern was developed during the early 1970s, long before more modern midge larvae and pupae began appearing in books and magazines. The original wool yarn is difficult to find, but just about any material of a gray-brown shade can be substituted.

Red Ass Willy

Hook: 1XL or 2XL, size 12-16
Tail: Four-strand floss, red
Body: Red floss
Rib: One strand of peacock herl
Originator: Ken Magee

Wee Willy

Hook: 1XL nymph hook, size 12-16
Tail: Olive hackle fibers
Body: Red floss
Rib: Peacock herl
Hackle: Two turns of olive saddle hackle, tied wet-fly style and trimmed short

Henry's Lake Renegade (Fore & Aft)

Hook: 1XL or 2XL nymph hook, size 8-14
Rear Hackle: One or two turns of brown hackle
Body: Peacock herl, sparse and thin
Rib: Red 3/0 thread counter-wrapped over peacock herl
Front Hackle: One or two turns of brown hackle

Canadian Brown Leech

Hook: 3-4XL streamer hook, size 2-12
Tail: Brown marabou (optional)
Body: Brown Mohair, wrapped and then picked out
Notes: The Mohair used to tie this pattern was originally called Canadian Mohair Yarn, hence the name of this pattern, whose origins are not entirely clear. Nonetheless, the fly likely originated in southern Idaho and not, as other writers have suggested, in Canada. For a time, the fine Mohair was difficult to obtain, but owing to the explosive growth of the fly-tying materials trade, Mohair is relatively easy to obtain now. Another popular color variation is the Canadian Blood Leech, which uses the maroon or wine shade of Mohair. By using two strands of Mohair, each of a different color, you can create the illusion of mixed shade Mohair simply picking the hair out with a bodkin or pick. Good combinations include brown/olive, brown/blood, black/purple, tan/olive, tan/brown. The addition of a marabou tail is another option, whose origination likely postdates the original fly only by a short period. Dave Tucker notes that the Canadian Brown Leech is the fore-runner for all of the Mohair leech patterns and for the very similar dubbed patterns that followed.

California Leech

Hook: 3XL streamer hook, size 2-12
Tail: Brown marabou with 3-4 strands of brown or black Krystal Flash
Underbody: Black or brown Krystal Flash
Body: Canadian brown Mohair or similar dubbing, loop dubbed so that underbody shows through
Originator: Bill Schiess

Halloween Leech

Hook: 3XL streamer, size 4-12
Tail: Black marabou
Body: Burnt orange/black variegated chenille
Hackle: Grizzly dyed hot orange, palmered through body
Notes: Bill Schiess developed this pattern during the days when the famed Canadian brown Mohair was scarce and difficult to obtain.

Green Halloween

Notes: Same as above but use chartreuse/black variegated chenille for the body and black saddle for the hackle. Originated by Bill Schiess.

Olive Damsel Nymph

Hook: 2XL nymph hook, size 8-14
Tail: Light olive marabou
Abdomen: Light olive wool yarn
Wingcase: Pheasant tail fibers
Thorax: Light olive chenille

Pheasant Rump Damsel

Hook: 2XL nymph hook, size 8-14
Tail: Olive-dyed pheasant rump marabou fibers
Body: Olive-dyed pheasant rump marabou cut off the quill and loop dubbed
Notes: A Ken Magee creation, this fly dates to the early 1970s. In keeping with typical southern Idaho tradition, the dye lot used for this fly has been a long-kept secret. Dave Tucker says that the "wrong color will catch fish, but the original kills them."

Pheasant Tail Damsel

Hook: 2XL nymph hook, size 8-14
Tail: 5-6 pheasant tail fibers
Abdomen: Pheasant tail fibers wrapped on shank, thin
Wingcase: Pheasant tail fibers
Thorax: Light olive chenille
Legs: Brown hackle palmered through the thorax and trimmed short

Tuck's Damsel

Hook: 2 or 3XL nymph hook, size 8-14
Tail: Tannish olive marabou
Abdomen: Tannish-olive marabou twisted and wrapped forward
Wingcase: Olive-dyed pheasant tail fibers
Thorax: Light olive rabbit or seal fur dubbing
Eyes: Plastic bead chain
Head: Same dubbing as thorax, with pheasant tail fibers pulled over to form a shell on top
Originator: Dave Tucker

Six Pack

Hook: 1 or 2XL nymph hook, size 8-12
Tail: Gold-dyed pheasant rump fibers
Body: Gold-dyed pheasant rump hackle, tied in by the tip, then twisted counter-clockwise and wrapped forward
Hackle: Gold-dyed pheasant rump hackle tied wet-fly style
Notes: First appearing on the lakes of eastern Washington, this fly soon drifted into the stillwater angling fraternity of southern Idaho.

Black Chironomid

Hook: 1 or 2XL, size 10-16
Rib: Flat silver tinsel
Body: Black rabbit dubbing
Head: White rabbit fur
Notes: A long-time favorite on the trout lakes of eastern Washington, this fly also has become standard issue in southern Idaho.

Suspender Midge

Hook: Curved scud hook, light wire, size 10-22
Body: Black Flashabou, 2-3 strands wrapped on shank
Thorax: Black poly dubbing
Wing: White poly yarn or Z-lon tied as a post
Hackle: Grizzly dry-fly hackle, tied parachute
Notes: Dave Tucker says, "this fly came to us via an English magazine. The original was rather crude, but a few of us (Tucker, Ken Magee, John Hull) saw the possibilities."

Henry's Lake Leech

Hook: 3-4XL streamer, size 4-10
Tail: Rusty brown marabou
Body: Tobacco brown chenille or brown/olive variegated chenille
Hackle: Brown hackle, palmered through body and then clipped short
Optional: Bend hook slightly upwards at mid-shank to help the fly twist and turn in the water.
Notes: Dave Tucker notes that the trimmed hackle on this and other such flies accomplishes a more streamlined appearance and also helps the fly trap air bubbles on the first few casts. The version tied with the olive-brown variegated chenille, to my knowledge, is a variation first offered by Jimmy Gabettas in the 1970s.

Bell Rapids Leech (Black & Tan)

Hook: 3-4XL streamer, size 6-12
Tail: Dark brown or black marabou
Body: Variegated tan/black chenille

Water Boatman

Hook: 1XL nymph hook, size 10-14
Shellback: Natural turkey tail
Body: Peacock herl, tied fat
Legs: One pair of black rubber legs tied half-way in the body, sticking out to the sides like oars
Notes: Originated by Rupe Gates. Dave Tucker notes that although Rupe Gates was not himself a tier, he did devise a few effective patterns. "This one," Tucker says, "sold very well over the years."

Trueblood Otter Nymph

Hook: 1XL nymph, size 8-18
Tail: Partridge hackle fibers
Body: Otter fur dubbing
Rib: Fine copper wire
Throat: Partridge fibers
Notes: This Ted Trueblood creation took advantage of the plumage of the Hungarian partridge, which had been introduced as a game bird in southern Idaho and thrives there to this day. Despite waning in popularity over the years, this pattern remains a great producer.

Pheasant Tail Crawdad

Hook: 3XL streamer hook, size 2-8
Tail: Two bunches of pheasant tail fibers separated at the rear to form a "V" to represent pincers
Body: Olive chenille
Shellback: Pheasant tail fibers
Legs: Brown hackle palmered over the rear of the body before the shellback is pulled over
Rib: Black 3/0 thread wrapped over the front half of the body after the shellback is pulled forward
Head: Leave the pheasant tail fibers protruding over the eye of the hook and trim them in a fan-shape to mimic tail
Originator: Marv Taylor

Flies for Idaho Trout Streams: Selected Dressings (tied by Dave Tucker except where noted)

Stonefly Patterns

Foam Head Stone

Hook: Long shank dry fly, size 2-10
Body: Golden-yellow poly dubbing (or to match natural)
Shellback: Gray closed-cell foam strip (e.g. Larva Lace Foam Strip)
Rib: Yellow size "A" monocord thread
Underwing: Olive Z-lon or similar
Wing: Light elk hair
Head: Gray closed-cell foam strip, one tied on top and one tied on bottom, both pulled forward
Legs: One pair of medium gray or brown rubber legs tied in at middle of head X-fashion before foam is pulled forward and tied down

Notes: Originated by Spank Warner, this uncomplicated and effective dressing can be modified in size and color to imitate virtually any adult stonefly

Marcella's Trout Fly

Hook: Long shank dry fly, size 4-6
Tail: Light elk hair, stacked
Body: Fluorescent orange yarn
Rib: Brown saddle hackle palmered through body
Wing: Natural brown bucktail
Hackle: Dark furnace, tied full

Notes: Traditionally, this pattern was perhaps the most popular giant stonefly imitation in use in eastern Idaho. Locally celebrated tier Marcella Oswald developed the pattern during the 1950s and subsequently sold thousands of dozens of them through the next few decades. For a more complete history, see Bruce Staples book, *Snake River Country*. When I lived in eastern Idaho during the 1970s, this fly, along with the Sofa Pillow, was the only salmonfly pattern known to me, because of the full bins at Pond's Lodge labeled "Trout Fly."

Lawson's Henry's Fork Stonefly (Bullet-Head Stone)

Hook: Long shank dry fly, size 4-8
Tail: Elk hair (or moose for salmonfly)
Body: Poly yarn, yellow or orange
Rib: Short brown hackle, palmered through body and counter-wrapped with fine wire
Wing: Natural light elk or deer

Head/Collar: Dyed yellow elk (golden stonefly) or dark elk (salmonfly) tied bullet style

Notes: Mike Lawson is something of an institution in eastern Idaho, as is his fly shop, Henry's Fork Anglers, Inc., located just across the highway from the banks of the Henry's Fork at Last Chance. The Henry's Fork Stonefly is just one of Lawson's many contributions to the list of effective Idaho trout patterns.

Mormon Girl, Dry

Hook: Dry fly, size 10-18
Tag: Red floss
Body: Yellow poly dubbing or floss
Rib: Grizzly hackle palmered through body
Wing: Light elk hair, down-wing style
Hackle: Grizzly

Notes: This classic Rocky Mountain trout pattern likely dates to the 1920s or 30s, perhaps earlier still. Bruce Staples offers an enlightening discussion of the pattern in his book, *Snake River Country*. The pattern is tied both wet and dry and although meant to imitate several species of small stoneflies, it has long been used as an effective general-use attractor pattern. The above dressing for a dry version comes from Dave Tucker and is superbly adapted to imitate the little yellow stoneflies that hatch on many Idaho trout streams. A more classic dry fly is created by tying divided Catskill-style wings of bronze mallard fibers along with the grizzly hackle.

Mormon Girl, Wet

Hook: Wet fly, size 10-16
Tag: Bright red floss
Body: Bright yellow floss
Rib: Fine silver flat tinsel
Hackle: Grizzly tied wet-fly style
Wing: Mallard flank or bronze mallard fibers, tied down-wing style

Little Yellow Sally

Hook: Tiemco #200 or similar, size 12-18
Tail: Bleached deer hair, tied short
Body: Yellowish olive (mustard) poly dubbing
Hackle: Light dun palmered through body
Wing: Bleached deer hair, tied low to the body
Hackle: Light dun tied as collar

Notes: Dave Tucker developed this pattern and suggests a second version with a bright yellow body, ginger hackle and red butt, the latter feature imitating the egg sack carried to the water by the ovipositing female insect.

Orange & Black Stonefly Nymph

Hook: Curved nymph hook (e.g. Tiemco #200), size 2-8
Tail: Black goose biots
Abdomen: Black and orange yarn, woven
Wingcase: Dark brown turkey tail
Legs: Brown partridge hackle pulled over thorax (under wingcase)
Thorax: Orange yarn, shredded and dubbed
Originator: Dave Tucker

Super "X"

Hook: 3XL or 4XL streamer hook
Tail: Black sparkle yarn
Body: Black chenille
Legs: One pair of white medium rubber legs tied in behind thorax
Thorax: Hot orange chenille
Hackle: White saddle

This Wes Newman creation is essentially an evolved version of the ever-popular Double Renegade and its inclusion in this section on stoneflies is testimony to the flies effectiveness when fished dead-drift prior to and during the salmonfly hatch on rivers like the South Fork Snake and Box Canyon of the Henry's Fork.

Bitch Creek

Hook: 3XL nymph hook, size 2-8 (example tied on Tiemco #200)
Tail: One pair of rubber legs material, white or black
Abdomen: Woven chenille, black on top, orange below
Thorax: Black chenille
Hackle: Dark furnace palmered through thorax
Antennae: White or black rubber legs, tied forward

Notes: The exact origin of this pattern seems to be lost to us, but it probably came from Montana, although there exist some fly anglers in eastern Idaho who will contend that the fly originated there and was named for the Bitch Creek that flows into the Teton River. While light orange is usually the accepted color, Dave Tucker's use of dark orange chenille in the abdomen makes for an improved version in my opinion.

Box Canyon Stone

Hook: 3XL nymph hook, size 2-6
Tail: Black or dark brown goose biots
Body: Black yarn, twisted to form segmented appearance
Wingcase: Dark turkey segment
Thorax: Black yarn
Hackle: Dark furnace palmered through thorax
Notes: According to Terry Hellekson, this pattern was originated in 1974 by Mims Barker of Ogden, Utah. For a golden stonefly nymph pattern, simply change the body color to medium brown or brownish-tan.

George's Brown Stone

Hook: 3XL nymph hook, size 4-10
Tail: Natural brown-gray mink hair
Body: Woven of brown yarn (top) and natural tan burlap (bottom)
Legs: Mink fur spun as a collar, extending 1/3 to 1/2 body length
Notes: This George Anderson pattern can be altered slightly by adding white rubber legs front and rear and dubbing a thorax of gray rabbit blend.

Caddisfly Patterns

Elk Hair Caddis

Hook: Dry fly, size 10-20
Body: Fine dubbing to match naturals
Hackle: To match body color
Rib: Fine wire or thread counter-wrapped over hackle stem
Wing: Elk hair
Notes: Originated by Al Troth of Montana and now subject to endless variations in color and theme, including the Deer Hair Caddis, a version that many tiers, myself included, tied early on simply because deer hair was more available than elk hair.

Lawson's Spent Partridge Caddis

Hook: Dry fly, size 12-18
Body: Dubbing to match natural (common shades include olive, green, gray, amber, tan)
Wings: Two partridge hackle tips, tied low and slightly overlapping in a spent position
Thorax: Fine peacock herl
Hackle: One grizzly and one brown hackle, wrapped through thorax and clipped flush top and bottom
Notes: This Mike Lawson original dates to the 1970s and has proven its effectiveness on both the flat waters of Harriman Park and the gliding runs and tailouts of other sections of the Henry's Fork. It is equally effective on any river where caddis are prevalent.

South Fork Caddis, Light

Hook: Dry fly, size 12-22
Body: Dark tan Australian opossum dubbing
Wing: Brown partridge feather tied flat over the back and topped with a sparse bunch of tan deer hairs
Hackle: Medium blue dun
Originator: John Hull

South Fork Caddis, Dark

Hook: Dry fly, size 12-22
Body: Dark gray Australian opossum dubbing
Wing: Dark gray turkey flat or duck shoulder tied flat over the body and topped with a sparse bunch of dark deer hairs
Hackle: Dark dun or black
Originator: John Hull

X-Caddis

Hook: Dry fly, size 12-20
Tail: Sparse length of Z-lon or similar tied as a trailing shuck
Body: Dubbing to match natural
Wing: Elk or deer hair, tied short to mimic emerging wings

Notes: This Craig Mathews creation is one of the best all-around patterns for use during caddis emergences, wherein trout often concentrate more on emerging pupae than on the adults. Simply alter the size and color of the pattern to match various caddis hatches.

Olive Beadhead

Hook: 1XL nymph hook, size 8-18
Body: Twisted Z-lon (light olive)
Thorax: Pearl Lite Brite, dubbed (keep thorax short)
Head: Silver bead
Notes: This pattern, submitted by Dave Tucker, makes an excellent imitation of the free-living *Rhyacophila* caddis larva (green rockworms found in many Western rivers).

Bead Caddis larva

Hook: 1XL nymph hook, size 10-16
Body: Brown Australian opossum dubbing
Thorax: Two plastic beads, olive or tan
Head: Black hare's ear dubbing
Originator: John Hull

Mayfly Patterns

Sparkle-Dun

Hook: Dry fly, size 10-22
Tail: Z-lon as a trailing shuck
Body: Fine dubbing to match natural
Wing: Deer hair, tied Compara-dun style (upright and fanned)
Notes: This Craig Mathews pattern borrows everything from the popular Compara-dun save the tail, which in the Sparkle Dun takes the form of a trailing shuck. This pattern can be adapted to virtually any mayfly hatch simply by adjusting the size and color.

Parachute *Baetis*

Hook: Dry fly, size 16-22
Tails: Two dun Micro Fibetts, divided
Body: Olive dubbing to match natural
Wing: Dark dun turkey flat fibers tied as a post
Hackle: Dark dun, tied parachute-style

Notes: This effective basic parachute design can be used to tie imitations of most mayflies and is especially suited to riffles, glides and back-eddies where lightly dressed spring-creek-style dressings would sink.

Red Quill

Hook: Dry fly, size 14-22
Tail: Dark dun hackle fibers
Body: Stripped peacock herl, dyed deep red (or similar)
Wings: Lemon wood duck, divided and upright (Catskill style)
Hackle: Dark dun

Pink Cahill

Hook: Dry fly, size 14-20
Tail: Light ginger hackle fibers
Body: Pinkish-tan dubbing
Wings: Lemon wood duck, divided and upright (Catskill style)
Hackle: Light cream or light ginger

Notes: The Pink Cahill is a color adaptation of the classic Light Cahill and is used specifically to imitate the pink Albert mayflies (*Epeorus albertae*) that hatch on several Idaho streams, most notably the South Fork Boise and South Fork Snake. Dave Tucker notes that this version was created by Pete Hidy.

Pink Cahill Parachute

Hook: Dry fly, size 14-20
Tails: Tan Micro Fibetts, divided
Body: Pinkish-tan dubbing
Wing: Tan or white turkey flat fibers tied as a post
Hackle: Ginger, tied parachute style
Originator: Dave Tucker

CDC Dun

Hook: Dry fly, size 12-20
Tails: Micro-Fibetts, divided
Body: Turkey biots of appropriate color
Thorax: Poly dubbing or similar to match natural
Wing: 4-5 tufts of CDC flared like a Compara-dun wing

Notes: This versatile pattern can be adapted in size and color to match virtually any mayfly dun. Two useful colors on Idaho waters include tan or light gray wing and pinkish-tan body for pink Alberts; light gray or white wing and light green or yellow-green body for PMDs. Renowned Idaho fly designer Rene' Harrop was among the first to offer a series of simple and lhighly effective CDC patterns, many of which are especially well-suited to fishing the flat waters of Harriman Park and Silver Creek.

Pink CDC Emerger

Hook: Dry fly, size 14-20
Tails: White or ginger Micro Fibetts, divided
Abdomen: Tan or pink turkey biot
Thorax: Tannish-orange poly dubbing
Wing: 3-4 CDC feathers tied wet-fly style
Head: Same as thorax, over top of wing butts

Notes: This is a Dave Tucker dressing of a basic CDC emerger pattern whose color and size can be altered to match many different mayflies. It is especially useful on flat waters and on hatches of PMDs, *Baetis*, mahogany duns and slate-winged olives.

Lawson PMD CDC Emerger

Hook: Dry fly, size 14-18
Tail: Brown Z-lon as a trailing shuck (sparse)
Abdomen: Natural pheasant tail fibers counter-ribbed with fine wire
Thorax: Pale yellow poly dubbing
Wing: Tuft of gray CDC plumes extending back over the body
Legs: A few partridge fibers tied along the bottom edge of both sides of the wing
Head: Same as thorax
Originator: Mike Lawson

Mahogany Dun Emergent Cripple

Hook: Dry fly, size 16
Tail: Sparse tuft of brown Z-lon or similar
Body: Mahogany dubbing
Wings: Sparse tufts of gray Z-lon or CDC, tied short and delta-style
Thorax: Same as body
Hackle: Two turns of dark dun in front of wings and through dubbing, clipped flush below (finish dubbed thorax after hackle is tied down)

Notes: This was the first of my Emergent Cripple series and to this day remains my favorite pattern for fishing the mahogany dun hatch on the Henry's Fork. This fly can be tied in different colors and sizes to match other mayfly hatches, including PMDs, slate-winged olives and *Callibaetis*.

PMD Hackle Spinner

Hook: Dry fly, size 14-18
Tail: Micro Fibetts, divided
Body: Fine dubbing, pale olive or pale rust
Wings: Mix of dun and grizzly hackle, 2 turns each
Thorax: Same as abdomen, with fine dubbing strand wrapped through the hackles (then clip the hackle fibers flush below and nearly flush above)

Notes: This has long been my favorite pattern for fishing the PMD spinner falls on Silver Creek and the Henry's Fork. To tie the *Callibaetis* version, mix dark dun with grizzly for the hackle and change the body color to pale ash gray or light grayish-tan (size 14-16). For Trico Hackle Spinner, use black mole fur dubbing for the thorax, white or olive thread for the abdomen and white hackle for the wings (size 18-22).

Attractor Dry Flies, Terrestrial Patterns & Chironomid Patterns

Z-Lon Midge

Hook: Dry fly, size 16-22
Body: Black Flashabou
Wing: White Z-lon tied over the body (down-wing)
Thorax: Black poly dubbing
Hackle: Grizzly palmered through thorax

Griffith's Gnat

Hook: Dry fly, size 14-22
Body: Peacock herl
Hackle: Grizzly palmered through body
Rib: Counter-rib of fine wire or thread (optional)

Royal Wulff

Hook: Dry fly, size 10-20
Tail: Moose hair or elk hock
Body: 1/3 peacock herl, 1/3 red floss, 1/3 peacock herl
Wings: White calf tail or similar, upright and divided
Hackle: Brown, tied full

H & L Variant

Hook: Dry fly, size 10-18
Tail: White calf tail
Body: 2/3 stripped peacock herl; front 1/3 peacock herl
Wings: White calf tail or similar, upright and divided
Hackle: Brown, tied full

Royal Humpy

Hook: Dry fly, size 8-20
Tail: Moose or elk hock
Body: Red floss with moose or elk pulled over
Wings: White calf tail or similar, upright and divided
Hackle: Coachman brown, tied full
Notes: The Royal Humpy is just one popular version of the ever-useful Humpy series of flies. Color variations in this fly are as far-reaching as the mind can imagine. Keep a few Royal Humpies and few other colors handy and you can catch fish just about anywhere.

Double Humpy

Hook: 2XL or 3XL, size 6-10
Tail: Deer or elk hair
Overbody: Deer or elk hair
Underbody: Yellow, red or green monocord
Wings: Deer or elk, upright and divided
Hackles: Grizzly
Originator: Joe Allen

Royal Trude (as per fly plate)

Hook: Dry fly, size 8-18
Tail: None
Body: 1/2 peacock herl, 1/2 red floss
Thorax: Peacock herl in equal proportion to herl at rear of fly
Wing: Light elk, tied low over the body
Hackle: Light furnace or honey badger, tied through the thorax
Notes: This is a Dave Tucker variation of the Coachman Trude and one that no doubt fishes as well or better than the original.

St. Joe Special

Hook: Dry fly, size 10-18
Tag: Flat gold tinsel (optional)
Tail: Golden pheasant tippet fibers
Body: Kelly green floss
Wing: Grizzly hackle tips, upright and divided
Hackle: Grizzly
Notes: The most famous fly originating in the Idaho Panhandle, the St. Joe Special or St. Joe Favorite, as it is called by many, comes in several variations, any one of them being the "original" dressing depending upon who you happen to ask. Joe Roope, owner of the Castaway Fly Shop in Coeur d'Alene, offers four alternate dressings for the fly, the other three being: 1. gray floss body, gray duck quill wings. 2. burnt orange floss body. 3. chartreuse floss body. To confuse the matter even more, I might add that I once encountered an old-timer on the St. Joe who was fishing yet another version: green floss body ribbed with fine flat gold tinsel and a palmered grizzly hackle.

Cranefly Skater

Hook: 2XL, fine-wire dry-fly hook, size 6-14
Tail: Light elk hair
Body: Sandy tan poly dubbing
Hackle: Ginger saddle hackle wrapped fully over the body
Wing: Light elk hair spun around the hook so long ends form a collar facing slightly forward
Notes: Dave Tucker recommends this pattern for the cranefly hatch on the South Fork Boise.

Tucker's Foam Cricket

Hook: 1XL dry fly, size 4-10
Body: Black foam sheet material
Hackle: Grizzly
Wing: Medium natural tan elk hair
Head: Same as body, with foam pulled back and tied down at the collar
Legs: Orange rubber legs (medium) tied in X-fashion at collar
Notes: This deadly pattern was devised by Dave Tucker to imitate the black cicada's that hatch along the South Fork of the Boise during the summer. When they end up in the water, they offer a big mouthful that trout can't resist.

Krystal Ant

Hook: Dry fly, size 12-18
Body: Two distinct balls of black dubbing
Hackle: 2-3 turns of black
Wing: A few strands of pearl Krystal Flash

Dave's Hopper

Hook: 2XL or 3XL dry fly, size 4-12
Tail: Poly yarn
Body: Poly yarn (yellow, cream, olive, etc.)
Hackle: Brown saddle, clipped short and palmered over body
Wing: Turkey quill segment, laucquered and tied over body
Legs: Pheasant tail fibers, several to a bunch, knotted to form kicking legs and tied alongside body
Collar: Deer hair, spun
Head: Spun and clipped deer hair
Originator: Dave Whitlock

Bullet Head Hopper

Hook: 2XL dry fly, size 4-10
Tail: Short loop of poly yarn
Body: Poly yarn (yellow, olive, etc.)
Hackle: Brown saddle clipped short and palmered over body
Underwing: Golden pheasant tippet fibers
Wing: Turkey quill segment, lacquered and tied in over body
Head: Deer or elk, tied forward then pulled back to form bullet-style head and collar

Notes: While I'm not sure who originated the bullet-style head for hoppers and stoneflies, it is certain that Mike Lawson can be credited at the very least with popularizing the style in eastern Idaho.

Turck's Tarantula

Hook: 3XL, size 4-12
Tail: Amherst pheasant tippet
Body: Hare's ear dubbing
Underwing: White calf tail
Overwing: Pearl Krystal Flash
Collar: Spun deer hair
Legs: White or brown rubber legs
Head: Spun and clipped deer hair

Notes: Originated by Guy Turck as a beefed-up knock-off of the Madam-X, this fly has gained popularity on the South Fork of the Snake. Following Turck's lead, South Fork regulars fish the fly dead-drift, then swing the fly across the flow at the end of the drift, adding a few rod pumps, and then retrieve it back.

Chernobyl Ant

Hook: 3XL, size 4-8
Body: Tan foam below, black foam above (or other combinations)
Hackle: Brown (optional)
Legs: Black medium round rubber legs
Indicator: Yellow or orange strip of foam tied on top

Notes: Originated by Emmett Heath to imitate the big Mormon crickets found along the Green River in Utah, the Chernobyl Ant has gained considerable popularity on the South Fork of the Snake and other Idaho streams.

Streamers, Wet Flies & Nymphs

Renegade

Hook: Standard wet fly, size 8-18
Tag: Flat gold tinsel
Rear Hackle: Brown, tied wet-fly style
Body: Peacock herl
Front Hackle: White, tied wet-fly style

Notes: The ever-popular Renegade was originated in the 1930s by Taylor "Beartracks" Williams of Sun Valley. This fly has long been one of the most popular flies in Idaho and is tied both dry and wet, the difference being the quality of hackle used. To increase durability, counter-rib the herl with fine wire or twist the herl into the thread.

Super Renegade

Hook: 2XL or 3XL streamer hook, size 2-10
Tag: Flat gold tinsel (optional)
Hackles: Grizzly, one at the rear, one at the joint (middle), one at the front
Body: Rear half, olive chenille, one half brown chenille

Notes: This is just one of many color combinations for this popular South Fork Snake River pattern developed in 1959 by Ardell Jeppsen. The original dressing features a white hackle at front, brown hackle at the joint and grizzly hackle at the rear; the body was peacock herl at the front and white chenille at the rear. Popular contemporary variations include shades of pink, purple, black, white and just about every possible combination of shades. The fly is typically fished streamer style on a sink-tip line and has even taken its share of trout on area still waters like Henry's Lake and Island Park Reservoir.

Kiwi Muddler

Hook: 3XL or 4XL streamer hook, size 2/0-6
Tail: Gray squirrel tail fibers
Body: Tan yarn
Rib: Oval gold tinsel
Wing: Wide rabbit strip cut in an elongated diamond shape
Head/Collar: Spun deer hair
Originator: Jack Dennis

Zonker

Hook: 3XL or 4XL streamer hook, size 2/0-6
Body: Mylar tubing (gold, pearl or silver) over under body form of "Zonker tape" if desired (body can be coated with epoxy to make a more durable fly)
Wing: Rabbit strip, tied in at front and tied down at rear of body
Hackle: Grizzly, tied in before wing is secured
Originator: Dan Byford

Fizzler

Hook: 1XL or 2XL wet fly, size 4-8
Tail: Orange goose quill fibers
Body: Peacock-green chenille with a single strand of light orange chenille pulled under the body
Hackle: Grizzly saddle palmered through the body

Notes: Another eastern Idaho pattern, this one was created in the 1940s by Etsel Radford, primarily for the South Fork Snake, where it can be dead-drifted on a floating or sink-tip line or quartered across and retrieved on a high-density sink-tip line.

Double Bunny

Hook: Bass Bug Hook (Tiemco size 8089)
Body: Diamond Braid (pearl, gold or silver)
Wing: Rabbit strips, dark color above, lighter color underneath hook shank, both strips glued to the body with Zap-a-Gap or Barge Cement.
Eyes: 7 or 8mm plastic doll eyes glued on the sides with Goop or soft head cement

Notes: Originated by Scott Sanchez of Livingston, Montana, this streamer pattern is used with regularity on the South Fork Snake in Wyoming, but is also gaining popularity on the Idaho side, especially with anglers in pursuit of brown trout on the lower reaches.

Whitlock Sculpin

Hook: Salmon/steelhead hook or streamer hook, size 2/0-6
Body: Angora goat or seal dubbing
Gills: Red lamb's wool or similar dubbed in front of body
Rib: Silver or gold oval
Wing: Four dyed grizzly or badger hackles tied Matuka-style
Fins: Mottle brown hen body feathers, one per side
Collar: Spun deer hair
Head: Spun and clipped deer hair forming flattened "shovel" shape
Colors: To mimic naturals (example is golden-yellow body, gold-tan wing, head mixed of natural, yellow and dyed-brown deer hair.)

Beadhead Pheasant Tail Nymph

Hook: 1XL or 2XL nymph, size 8-18
Tail: Pheasant tail fibers
Abdomen: Pheasant tail fibers
Rib: Fine wire, counter-wrapped
Thorax: Peacock herl
Head: Metal bead

Beadhead Prince Nymph

Hook: 1XL or 2XL nymph hook, size 8-14
Tail: Two dark biots
Body: Peacock herl
Rib: Fine gold oval, counter-wrapped
Collar: A few turns of brown hackle and two white biots extending over the back
Head: Metal bead

Beadhead Hare's Ear Nymph

Hook: Nymph hook, size 6-18
Tail: Partridge or pheasant tail fibers
Abdomen: Hare's ear dubbing
Rib: Gold oval tinsel
Thorax: Same as abdomen, loosely dubbed
Head: Metal bead

The Steelhead Flies of Dave Burns

Dave Burns is a talented dresser of elegant salmon and steelhead flies and a passionate devotee of the sport of steelhead fly angling. He develops patterns for his favorite Idaho steelhead streams, the Salmon River and its forks, which are readily accessible from Dave's home-base of McCall.

Mango Spey (Dave Burns)

Tag: Flat silver tinsel, forming underbody and a tag of two turns
Body: Rear half fluorescent magenta or fluorescent pink floss; front half equal parts of light yellow, then gold seal dubbing or substitute
Rib: Flat silver tinsel, small oval silver and a counter of gold wire
Hackle: Fluorescent chartreuse marabou tied through body
Collar: Hen or cock hackle in deep fluorescent hot pink
Wing: Built wing of goose shoulder fibers married as follows: 4 fibers chartreuse, 1 fiber purple, 2 fibers red, 2 fibers orange, 2 yellow, 2 orange, 2 red, 1 purple, 4 chartreuse (mounted tent-style)
Head: Orange thread

Sunset Spey (Dave Burns)

Tag: Fine silver oval and magenta silk
Tail: Golden pheasant crest, dyed fluorescent pink and Chinese kingfisher rump
Butt: Ostrich herl, dyed lavender
Body, rear half: Light claret silk ribbed with small gold oval tinsel and veiled with kingfisher
Joint: Ostrich herl, dyed lavender
Body, front half: Purple silk ribbed with flat silver and oval silver
Hackle: Tied Spey style through front half of body— blue-eared pheasant or similar, dyed purple
Collar: Blue peacock breast
Wing: Built wing of goose shoulder fibers, married as follows: 4 purple, 4 blue, 1 purple, 2 red, 1 purple, 4 blue, 4 purple (mounted tent-tyle)

Rainbow Warrior (Dave Burns)

Tag: Small silver oval and fluorescent yellow silk
Tail: Golden pheasant crest topped with imitation Indian crow

Butt: Black ostrich herl
Body, rear half: Fluorescent orange floss ribbed with fine silver lace, fine silver flat tinsel and hackled with fluorescent pink golden pheasant crest
Joint: Black ostrich
Body, front half: Fluorescent red floss ribbed with medium silver oval and medium flat silver tinsel, hackled with purple-dyed golden pheasant crest
Collar: Black heron substitute (e.g. ringneck pheasant or blue-eared pheasant dyed black)
Cheeks: Jungle cock, tilted down
Wing: Built wing of single goose shoulder fibers married as follows with single fiber of black between each (top to bottom): purple, royal blue, kingfisher blue, green, yellow, orange, red; mounted tent-style

Red Pheasant (Dave Burns)

Tag: Fine gold oval and lavender silk
Tail: Golden pheasant crest, dyed hot pink
Butt: Ostrich dyed purple
Body: 1/5 light claret/magenta silk; front 4/5 violet silk
Rib: Medium gold oval
Hackle: Tragopan pheasant crest following rib over violet silk and countered with fine gold oval
Collar: Four golden pheasant flank feathers, with the shorter fibers removed
Wing: Matching slips from the tail feather of a tragopan pheasant
Head: Black

Lightning & Thunder (Dave Burns)

Tag: Flat silver
Tail: Two golden pheasant crests and red hackle tips veiled with jungle cock
Body, rear half: Gold flat tinsel ribbed with small gold oval, veiled above and below with red hackle tips
Body, front half: Black floss ribbed with gold oval and flat gold, hackled with orange heron substitute
Collar: Eurasian blue jay or guinea dyed kingfisher blue
Wings: Brown turkey tail slips, tied tent-style

Salmon River Red (Dave Burns)

Tag: Silver oval
Body: 1/5 bright claret silk, 4/5 claret wool
Rib: Flat silver Mylar tinsel overlaid with fluorescent magenta silk and edged at the rear by fine silver oval; counter-ribbed with fine silver oval
Hackle: Purple heron substitute, through body
Throat: Guinea, dyed red
Wing: Bronze mallard

South Fork Salmon River Spey (Dave Burns)

Tag: Silver oval
Body: 1/5 purple silk, 4/5 black wool
Rib: Same as for Salmon River Red
Hackle: Purple heron substitute, through body
Throat: Black & white speckled
Wing: Bronze mallard

Jean's Iris Spey (Dave Burns)

Tag: Silver oval
Body: 1/5 purple silk, 4/5 green wool
Rib: Same as for Salmon River Red Spey, except substitute fluorescent green silk
Hackle: Purple heron substitute
Throat: Guinea dyed green
Wing: Bronze mallard, dyed purple

Jean's Green Spey (Dave Burns)

Tag: Silver oval
Body: 1/5 green silk, 4/5 green wool
Rib: Same as Jean's Iris Spey
Hackle: Gray heron substitute
Throat: Guinea, dyed green
Wing: Bronze mallard

Salmon River Purple Skunk (Dave Burns)

Tag: Silver oval
Tail: Golden pheasant crest
Butt: Fluorescent yellow wool
Body: Purple silk
Rib: Small silver oval
Wing: Oscillated turkey, peacock sword, bronze mallard and a topping
Throat: Black

Psychedelic Green Butt Skunk (Dave Burns)

Tag: Silver flat tinsel
Tail: Golden pheasant crest, dyed fluorescent red
Body: 1/2 fluorescent chartreuse floss, 1/2 black seal dubbing or similar
Rib: Medium flat silver edged with fine silver oval
Hackle: Black cock hackle through front half of body
Throat: Black mallard rump
Wing: Built wing of goose shoulder, married as follows (top to bottom): 5 white, 1 black, 4 white, 2 black, 3 white, 3 black, 2 white, 4 black, 1 white, 5 black; and jungle cock

Deer Creek Royal Coachman (Dave Burns)

Hook: Alec Jackson Spey Hook, gold
Tag: Flat silver tinsel
Tail: Golden pheasant crest and tippet fibers
Body: 1/6 peacock herl, 4/6 golden yellow silk, 1/6 peacock herl
Rib: Fine gold oval as a counter
Throat: Golden pheasant rump
Wing: Plain cinnamon turkey with jungle cock over and three toppings

Steelhead Flies of Ray Watkins

Ray Watkins was a native of Idaho and lived there his entire life; he worked as a saw-filer at local mills and in the words of Dave Burns was a "true Western fly fishing gentleman in the best sense of the word." Watkins' elegantly simple steelhead dressings were used to good effect on the Salmon River. The flies were never named by their originator, so Dave Burns, who tied the examples, offers the dressings as numbers 1 through 4.

Ray Watkins, number 1

Tail: Black hair (bucktail, black bear or squirrel) tied long
Body: Alternating bands of orange and fluorescent flame wool yarn
Hackle: Palmered barred Plymouth rock cock hackle

Ray Watkins, number 2

Tail: Black hair
Body: Black wool or dubbing
Wing: Bucktail, dyed yellow

Ray Watkins, number 3

Tail: White hair
Body: Black wool or dubbing
Collar: Brown bucktail over white bucktail

Ray Watkins, number 4

Tail: White hair
Body: Red dubbing or wool
Wing: Bucktail, dyed yellow

Steelhead Flies of the Clearwater River

Most of the steelhead flies commonly in use on the Clearwater River are patterns borrowed from other regions. Naturally they produce as well on the Clearwater as on their home waters. However, quite a number of patterns, some of them variations on older dressings from the Pacific Coast, have been developed over the past few decades by anglers who live on or near the Clearwater and who frequent her wide pools. For an account of Clearwater flies and their originators, see Trey Combs' book *Steelhead Fly Fishing*.

Ward's Wasp

Tail: Golden pheasant tippet fibers
Butt: Yellow chenille
Body: Black chenille
Rib: Flat silver tinsel
Hackle: Yellow
Wing: Black or brown hair
Originator: Ed Ward

Bloody Muddler

Tail: White calf tail
Body: Gold Diamond Braid or gold tinsel chenille
Underwing: Red calf tail
Wing: Grizzly hackle tips, face to face over underwing
Head/Collar: Spun deer hair; trim head rather large so the fly will skate
Originator: Leroy Hyatt

Purple Skunk

Tail: Gray squirrel tail, sparse
Butt: Fluorescent green chenille
Body: Purple chenille ribbed with oval silver tinsel
Wing: Sparse gray squirrel tail
Collar: Purple hackle
Originator: Keith Stonebreaker

Green Ant

Tail: Golden pheasant tippet, tied short
Butt: Peacock herl
Body: Fluorescent green floss
Hackle: Black
Wing: Gray squirrel tail, sparse
Notes: Originated by Mike Arhutick; generally tied low-water (reduced) style.

Steelhead Skater, Grizzly Hackle Peacock

Wing: Black moose hair, tied forward and divided on underside of hook
Tail: Black moose hair, tied long
Body: Peacock herl, counter-ribbed with fine wire
Hackle: Grizzly, palmered through body
Hackle: 3-4 grizzly hackles, wrapped behind and in front of wings
Notes: Originated by Bob Wagoner, the Steelhead Skater is also tied in several other color variations; a similar pattern, based on Wagoner's fly, is Leroy Hyatt's version incorporating a spun deer-hair body, which creates a superbly buoyant skater.

Cigar Butt

Tail: White calf tail
Wing: White calf tail protruding over the eye of the hook
Body: Spun deer hair, trimmed to form a fat cigar-shape
Throat: Dark moose hairs (optional)
Notes: Keith Stonebreaker, once a member of the Idaho Fish & Game Commission, was among the early pioneers in dry-fly steelheading on the Clearwater. His popular Cigar Butt is a simplified version of the Bomber of Atlantic salmon fame.

December Gold

Hook: Single or double, salmon/steelhead hook
Tail: Golden pheasant crest
Body: Hot orange dubbing
Hackle: Hot orange, palmered through body
Wing: Golden pheasant tippets, paired and tied low over the body
Originator: Craig Lannigan

Purple Sundowner

Tag: Flat silver tinsel
Tail: Purple hackle fibers
Body: Fluorescent orange wool yarn
Hackle: Purple, palmered through body
Wing: Pearl Krystal Flash
Collar: Purple hackle
Notes: Originated by Bob Wagoner of Lewiston, the Sundowner series includes several other color variations.